First World War

and Army of Occupation

War Diary

France, Belgium and Germany

35 DIVISION
106 Infantry Brigade
Prince of Wales's Own (West Yorkshire Regiment)
17th Battalion
22 August 1915 - 8 December 1917

WO95/2490/4

The Naval & Military Press Ltd
www.nmarchive.com
Published in association with The National Archives

Published by

The Naval & Military Press Ltd

Unit 10 Ridgewood Industrial Park,

Uckfield, East Sussex,

TN22 5QE England

Tel: +44 (0) 1825 749494

www.naval-military-press.com

www.nmarchive.com

This diary has been reprinted in facsimile from the original. Any imperfections are inevitably reproduced and the quality may fall short of modern type and cartographic standards.

Contents

Document type	Place/Title	Date From	Date To
Heading	WO95/2490/4		
Heading	35th Division 106th Infy Bde 17th Bn West Yorks Jan 1916-Dec 1917 Amalgamated With 15 Bn West Yorks 31 Div 93 Bde		
Heading	War Diary Of 17th (S) Battn. West Yorkshire Regt. From 24/1/16 To 29/2/16 Volume I		
War Diary	Leeds	00/12/1914	00/12/1914
War Diary	Leeds	00/06/1915	00/06/1915
War Diary	Leeds	28/09/1915	28/09/1915
War Diary	Leeds	00/06/1915	00/06/1915
War Diary	Chiseldon	22/08/1915	22/08/1915
War Diary	Perham Down	23/11/1915	23/11/1915
War Diary	Larkhill	02/12/1915	02/12/1915
War Diary	Perham Down	18/12/1915	31/01/1916
War Diary	Southampton	31/01/1916	31/01/1916
War Diary	Havre	01/02/1916	02/02/1916
War Diary	Blendecques	03/02/1916	03/02/1916
War Diary	Campagne	04/02/1916	09/02/1916
War Diary	Boeseghem	09/02/1916	17/02/1916
War Diary	Merville.	18/02/1916	18/02/1916
War Diary	Le Sart.	19/02/1916	19/02/1916
War Diary	W & Z Coys at Riez Bailleul and Pont Du Hem ? X & Y Coys in The Trenches	20/02/1916	21/02/1916
War Diary	W & Z Coys Look the Place of X & Y Coys & Vice Versa.	22/02/1916	22/02/1916
War Diary	W & Z Coys in Trenches. X & Y in Billets at Riez Bailleul and Pont Du Hem.	23/02/1916	23/02/1916
War Diary	Riez Bailleul. Pont Du Hem. & Trenches.	24/02/1916	24/02/1916
Miscellaneous	17th (S) Battalion. West Yorkshire Regiment. Appendix 1		
Heading	War Diary Of 17th (S) Battn. West Yorkshire Regiment. From 1st March 1916 To 31st March 1916. Volume 2		
War Diary	Le Sart.	01/03/1916	01/03/1916
War Diary	Le Sart and La Gorgue	02/03/1916	02/03/1916
War Diary	La Gorgue	03/03/1916	06/03/1916
War Diary	La Gorgue and Trenches.	07/03/1916	07/03/1916
War Diary	Trenches M.24.2.-M.29.3.	08/03/1916	10/03/1916
War Diary	Trenches M.24.2-M.29.3 and Pont Du Hem.	11/03/1916	11/03/1916
War Diary	Pont Du Hem.	12/03/1916	13/03/1916
War Diary	Pont Du Hem. and Paradis.	14/03/1916	14/03/1916
War Diary	Paradis	15/03/1916	18/03/1916
War Diary	Paradis and Merville	19/03/1916	19/03/1916
War Diary	Merville	20/03/1916	25/03/1916
War Diary	Merville and Neuf Berquin.	26/03/1916	26/03/1916
War Diary	Neuf Berquin and Trenches.	27/03/1916	27/03/1916
War Diary	Trenches (Petillon)	28/03/1916	29/03/1916
Miscellaneous	Riez Bailleul Pont Du Hem and Trenches.	25/02/1916	26/02/1916
War Diary	Trenches & Lesart.	27/02/1916	27/02/1916
War Diary	Le Sart.	28/02/1916	29/02/1916
War Diary	Trenches.	30/03/1916	30/03/1916

War Diary	Trenches and Fleurbaix.	31/03/1916	31/03/1916
Heading	War Diary Of 17th (S) Bn West Yorkshire Regiment. From 1st April 1916 to 30th April 1916 Volume 3.		
War Diary	Fleurbaix.	01/04/1916	03/04/1916
War Diary	Fleurbaix and Neuf Berquin.	04/04/1916	04/04/1916
War Diary	Neuf Berquin.	05/04/1916	06/04/1916
War Diary	Neuf Berquin and Estaires.	07/04/1916	07/04/1916
War Diary	Estaires.	08/04/1916	11/04/1916
War Diary	Estaires and Trenches. N.13.6-N.8.2.	12/04/1916	13/04/1916
Miscellaneous	Trenches	13/04/1916	14/04/1916
War Diary	Trenches and Estaires.	15/04/1916	15/04/1916
War Diary	Estaires and Croix Barbee	16/04/1916	16/04/1916
War Diary	Croix Barbee.	17/04/1916	19/04/1916
War Diary	Croix Barbee and Trenches.	20/04/1916	20/04/1916
War Diary	Trenches S53.S5.4. S.5.5. S.5.6. 17351. 17352. Area 1.	21/04/1916	23/04/1916
War Diary	Trenches S5.3. S5.4. S.5.5. S.5.6. 17351. 17352. Area 1. and Croix Barbee.	24/04/1916	24/04/1916
War Diary	Croix Barbee.	25/04/1916	27/04/1916
War Diary	Croix Barbee and Les Lobes.	28/04/1916	30/04/1916
Heading	War Diary of 17th (S) Battn. West Yorkshire Regt., From 1st June 1916 To 30th June 1916 Volume V.		
War Diary	Trenches Festubert.	01/06/1916	06/06/1916
War Diary	Trenches Festubert Left Sub Sector.	07/06/1916	11/06/1916
War Diary	Billets at R 13. Bethune	11/06/1916	13/06/1916
War Diary	Combined Sheet.	13/06/1916	15/06/1916
War Diary	Combined Sheet and Hingette. W 16.17.	16/06/1916	16/06/1916
War Diary	Hingette. W16.17. And E.4.	17/06/1916	17/06/1916
War Diary	E.4. Bethune Combined Sheet.	18/06/1916	27/06/1916
War Diary	Bethune	28/06/1916	30/06/1916
Heading	War Diary of 17th (S) Bn. West Yorkshire Regt, From, 1st May 1916 to 31st May 1916 Volume IV.		
War Diary	Les Lobes.	01/05/1916	05/05/1916
War Diary	Les Lobes and Trenches.	06/05/1916	06/05/1916
War Diary	Trenches.	07/05/1916	09/05/1916
War Diary	Trenches and Billets at Richebourg.	10/05/1916	10/05/1916
War Diary	Richebourg.	11/05/1916	13/05/1916
War Diary	Richebourg and Trenches.	14/05/1916	14/05/1916
War Diary	Trenches.	15/05/1916	17/05/1916
War Diary	Trenches & Billets Richebourg St Vaast.	18/05/1916	19/05/1916
War Diary	Richebourg St Vaast.	20/05/1916	22/05/1916
War Diary	Richebourg St Vaast La Croix Billets at R 13.	22/05/1916	23/05/1916
War Diary	Billets at R 13	23/05/1916	27/05/1916
War Diary	Billets at R 13. & Trenches.	28/05/1916	28/05/1916
War Diary	Trenches S221. S.28.1. S272. S.27.1 Trench Map Area G.	29/05/1916	29/05/1916
War Diary	Trenches Festubert Section Left Sub Sector.	30/05/1916	31/05/1916
Heading	106th Bde. 35th Div. War Diary 17th Battalion West Yorks Regiment 1st to 31st July 1916. Report On Operations 29/30th July in G.S. Diary		
Heading	War Diary of 17th (S) Battn. West Yorkshire Regt. From 1st July 1916 to 31st July 1916. Volume 6		
War Diary	Bethune	01/07/1916	02/07/1916
War Diary	Le Souich.	03/07/1916	05/07/1916
War Diary	Bois du Warnimont.	06/07/1916	09/07/1916
War Diary	Bois du Warnimont and Varemies. P 25.d. 3.7 Sheet 57.d.	10/07/1916	10/07/1916

War Diary	Varennes.	11/07/1916	12/07/1916
War Diary	Bresle & Bois des Celestines & Billon Copse.	13/07/1916	14/07/1916
War Diary	Talus Boise	14/07/1916	18/07/1916
War Diary	Talus Boise and South Trench. S27.d.	18/07/1916	18/07/1916
War Diary	South Trench S.27.d.	19/07/1916	20/07/1916
War Diary	Caftet Wood	21/07/1916	21/07/1916
War Diary	Caftet Wood and Nuch A 1.c.d.	22/07/1916	23/07/1916
War Diary	Trench A I.C.d. and Bernafay Wood	24/07/1916	24/07/1916
War Diary	Bernafay Wood	25/07/1916	25/07/1916
War Diary	Caftet Wood & Casewent Trench Casuneul ? & Caftet Wood	26/07/1916	27/07/1916
War Diary	Caftet Wood	28/07/1916	28/07/1916
War Diary	Caftet Wood and Dublie Geuel.	29/07/1916	29/07/1916
War Diary	Outhil Trench and Naltz Horn Farm Geudu	30/07/1916	30/07/1916
War Diary	Rollz Horn Farm Trench & Caftet Wood & Sandpit Valley	31/07/1916	31/07/1916
Heading	106th Brigade 35th Division. 1/17th Battalion West Yorks Regiment August 1916		
War Diary	1-8-T Sand Pit Valley. E & D Figa Sheet U 2 D N E.	01/08/1916	01/08/1916
War Diary	Morlancourt.	02/08/1916	05/08/1916
War Diary	Morlancourt and Train.	05/08/1916	05/08/1916
War Diary	Le Mesge	06/08/1916	09/08/1916
War Diary	Le Mesge and Train.	10/08/1916	10/08/1916
War Diary	Moflan Court	11/08/1916	15/08/1916
War Diary	Moflan Court & Sand Pit Valley	16/08/1916	16/08/1916
War Diary	Sand Pit Valley.	17/08/1916	19/08/1916
War Diary	Sand Pit Valley and Coulour Wood Camp T.24.C.	20/08/1916	22/08/1916
War Diary	Silesia Trench	23/08/1916	24/08/1916
War Diary	Selesca Trench & Front Line	24/08/1916	24/08/1916
War Diary	Front Line.	25/08/1916	27/08/1916
War Diary	Hepper Valley	28/08/1916	29/08/1916
War Diary	Happer Valley & Train	30/08/1916	30/08/1916
War Diary	Bernaville & Sus St Leger.	31/08/1916	31/08/1916
War Diary	Sus St Leger	01/09/1916	01/09/1916
War Diary	Sus St Leger & Hauteville	02/09/1916	05/09/1916
War Diary	Hauteville & Duisans	05/09/1916	05/09/1916
War Diary	Duisans	06/09/1916	08/09/1916
War Diary	Arras.	09/09/1916	09/09/1916
War Diary	Trenches K 1. Sector.	10/09/1916	16/09/1916
War Diary	Arras Roclincourt St Nicholas.	17/09/1916	21/09/1916
War Diary	Trenches K 1 Sector.	22/09/1916	27/09/1916
War Diary	Trenches K 1 Sector & Arras	28/09/1916	28/09/1916
War Diary	Arras	29/09/1916	04/10/1916
War Diary	Arras K 1 Sector	05/10/1916	07/10/1916
War Diary	K 1.	07/10/1916	10/10/1916
War Diary	K1 & Arras St Nicholas	11/10/1916	16/10/1916
War Diary	K 1	17/10/1916	22/10/1916
War Diary	K1 & Arras.	23/10/1916	23/10/1916
War Diary	Arras	24/10/1916	28/10/1916
War Diary	Arras & K 1.	29/10/1916	31/10/1916
War Diary	K 1	01/11/1916	03/11/1916
War Diary	K 1 Bde Res.	04/11/1916	09/11/1916
War Diary	K 1.	10/11/1916	15/11/1916
War Diary	K 1 & Arras	16/11/1916	16/11/1916
War Diary	Arras.	16/11/1916	21/11/1916
War Diary	K 1	22/11/1916	27/11/1916

War Diary	K 1 & Bde Res	28/11/1916	28/11/1916
War Diary	Bde Res	29/11/1916	30/11/1916
War Diary	Bde Res & Arras	01/12/1916	01/12/1916
War Diary	Arras	02/12/1916	31/12/1916
War Diary	Appendix 1.	04/12/1917	04/12/1917
War Diary	Appendix 2.	04/12/1917	04/12/1917
War Diary	Appendix 3.	04/12/1917	04/12/1917
War Diary	Appendix 4.	05/12/1917	05/12/1917
War Diary	Appendix 5	06/12/1917	06/12/1917
War Diary	Appendix 6	10/12/1917	10/12/1917
War Diary	Appendix 7	11/12/1917	11/12/1917
War Diary	Appendix 8	12/12/1917	12/12/1917
War Diary	Appendix 9	15/12/1917	15/12/1917
War Diary	Appendix 10	19/12/1917	19/12/1917
War Diary	Appendix 11	21/12/1917	21/12/1917
War Diary	Appendix 12	23/12/1917	23/12/1917
War Diary	Appendix 13	26/12/1917	26/12/1917
War Diary	Appendix 14	29/12/1917	29/12/1917
War Diary	Appendix 15		
War Diary	Ternas	01/01/1917	05/02/1917
War Diary	Ternas & Fortel	06/02/1917	06/02/1917
War Diary	Fortel & Outrebois	07/02/1917	07/02/1917
War Diary	Outebois & Havernas	08/02/1917	08/02/1917
War Diary	Havernas	09/02/1917	18/02/1917
War Diary	Havernas & Marcelcave	19/02/1917	19/02/1917
War Diary	Marcelcave	20/02/1917	21/02/1917
War Diary	Marcelcave & Caix	22/02/1917	22/02/1917
War Diary	Caix	23/02/1917	23/02/1917
War Diary	Caix & Camp des Ballons	24/02/1917	24/02/1917
War Diary	Camp Des Ballons	25/02/1917	25/02/1917
War Diary	Camp des Ballons & Trenches (Lihons Sector)	26/02/1917	26/02/1917
War Diary	Trenches	27/02/1917	28/02/1917
War Diary	Trenches Lihons Sector	01/03/1917	08/03/1917
War Diary	Lihons Sector	09/03/1917	10/03/1917
War Diary	Rosieres	11/03/1917	13/03/1917
War Diary	Rosieres & Decauville Camp	14/03/1917	14/03/1917
War Diary	Decauville Camp	15/03/1917	15/03/1917
War Diary	Decauville Camp & Chilly Sector	16/03/1917	16/03/1917
War Diary	Chilly Sector.	17/03/1917	18/03/1917
War Diary	Hallu	19/03/1917	28/03/1917
War Diary	Hallu & Potte	29/03/1917	29/03/1917
War Diary	Potte	30/03/1917	02/04/1917
War Diary	Potte Pargny & Falvy	03/04/1917	03/04/1917
War Diary	Pargny & Falvy	04/04/1917	04/04/1917
War Diary	Pargny & Falvy & Ennemain	05/04/1917	05/04/1917
War Diary	Ennemain	06/04/1917	08/04/1917
War Diary	Monchy La Gache & Tertry	09/04/1917	09/04/1917
War Diary	Vermand	10/04/1917	14/04/1917
War Diary	Trenches Pont Ru Area.	15/04/1917	18/04/1917
War Diary	Soyecourt	19/04/1917	30/04/1917
War Diary	Line Fresnoy-Gricourt Area	01/05/1917	04/05/1917
War Diary	Reserve Trenches Fresnoy Gricourt & St Quentin Art Wood	05/05/1917	08/05/1917
War Diary	Soyecourt	09/05/1917	18/05/1917
War Diary	Peronne	19/05/1917	20/05/1917
War Diary	Sorel Le Grand	21/05/1917	21/05/1917

War Diary	Trenches	22/05/1917	28/05/1917
War Diary	Villers Guislain	29/05/1917	02/06/1917
War Diary	Templeux La Fosse	03/06/1917	09/06/1917
War Diary	Line Villers Guislain Sector	10/06/1917	10/06/1917
War Diary	Villers Guislain Sector	11/06/1917	14/06/1917
War Diary	Camp Near Heudicourt	15/06/1917	21/06/1917
War Diary	Camp Near Heudicourt & Villers Guislain Sector	22/06/1917	22/06/1917
War Diary	Villers Guislain Sector	23/06/1917	26/06/1917
War Diary	Aizecourt Le Bas.	27/06/1917	01/07/1917
War Diary	Aizecourt Le Bas & Lieramont	02/07/1917	02/07/1917
War Diary	Lieramont	03/07/1917	06/07/1917
War Diary	C I Sub-Sector	07/07/1917	15/07/1917
War Diary	Quarries Templeux Le Guerard	16/07/1917	23/07/1917
War Diary	Aizecourt Le Bas	24/07/1917	31/07/1917
War Diary	Aizecourt Le Bas & Epehy Sector.	01/08/1917	01/08/1917
War Diary	Epehy Sector	02/08/1917	04/08/1917
War Diary	Lempire & Ronssoy	05/08/1917	06/08/1917
War Diary	Lempire & Ronssoy & Line	07/08/1917	07/08/1917
War Diary	Line	08/08/1917	10/08/1917
War Diary	Ronssoy	11/08/1917	13/08/1917
War Diary	Ronssoy & Line	14/08/1917	14/08/1917
War Diary	Line	15/08/1917	17/08/1917
War Diary	Lempire Ronssoy & Line.	18/08/1917	24/08/1917
War Diary	Villers Faucon & St Emilie	25/08/1917	25/08/1917
War Diary	St-Emilie	26/08/1917	26/08/1917
War Diary	The Knoll	27/08/1917	31/08/1917
War Diary	Villers Faucon & Aizecourt-Le-Bas	01/09/1917	01/09/1917
War Diary	Aizecourt-Le-Bas	02/09/1917	06/09/1917
War Diary	Bde Support E Of Epehy.	07/09/1917	11/09/1917
War Diary	Front Line (Birdcage)	12/09/1917	12/09/1917
War Diary	Birdcage Sector	13/09/1917	17/09/1917
War Diary	Birdcage Sector & Villers Faucon	18/09/1917	18/09/1917
War Diary	Villers Faucon	19/09/1917	25/09/1917
War Diary	Lempire.	26/09/1917	28/09/1917
War Diary	Lempire & Fleeceall & Grafton Posts.	29/09/1917	30/09/1917
War Diary	Fleeceall & E B O Posts. Bde H.Q.	01/10/1917	01/10/1917
War Diary	Lempire	02/10/1917	02/10/1917
War Diary	Villers Faucon	03/10/1917	03/10/1917
War Diary	Agnez Les Duisans.	04/10/1917	13/10/1917
War Diary	Rudbrook	14/10/1917	15/10/1917
War Diary	Bennet Camp.	16/10/1917	17/10/1917
War Diary	Wijdendrift	18/10/1917	20/10/1917
War Diary	Elverdinghe	20/10/1917	21/10/1917
War Diary	Elverdinghe & Vec Band Caduy	22/10/1917	23/10/1917
War Diary	Wijdendrift	24/10/1917	26/10/1917
War Diary	Boesinghe & Proven	27/10/1917	27/10/1917
War Diary	Proven	28/10/1917	29/10/1917
War Diary	Proven & De wippe	30/10/1917	30/10/1917
War Diary	De wippe	31/10/1917	31/10/1917
Miscellaneous	To D.A.G. Base	09/12/1917	09/12/1917
Heading	De Wippe Boesinghe & Elverdinghe	01/11/1917	01/11/1917
War Diary	Boesinghe	02/11/1917	03/11/1917
War Diary	Boesinghe & Proven	04/11/1917	04/11/1917
War Diary	Proven	05/11/1917	15/11/1917
War Diary	Elverdinghe	16/11/1917	30/11/1917
War Diary	Thieushoek	01/12/1917	01/12/1917

War Diary	Merville	02/12/1917	02/12/1917
War Diary	L'Ecleme	03/12/1917	03/12/1917
War Diary	Barlin	04/12/1917	04/12/1917
War Diary	Acq	05/12/1917	08/12/1917

WO95/2490/4

35TH DIVISION
106TH INFY BDE

17TH BN WEST YORKS

JAN ~~FEB~~ 1916-DEC 1917

AMALGAMATED WITH
15 BN WEST YORKS

31 DIV

93 BDE

2281

3/106
5

ORIGINAL.

CONFIDENTIAL

W A R D I A R Y

OF

17TH (S) BATTN. WEST YORKSHIRE REGT.

From .24/1/16....... To...29/2/16..........

VOLUME....I....

Instructions regarding War Diaries and Intelligence Summaries are contained in F. S. Regs., Part II. and the Staff Manual respectively. Title Pages will be prepared in manuscript.

WAR DIARY

or

~~INTELLIGENCE SUMMARY~~

(Erase heading not required.)

Army Form C. 2118

Place	Date	Hour	Summary of Events and Information	Remarks and references to Appendices
Leeds	12/14		17th (S) Battn. West Yorkshire Regiment raised in Leeds under Raisers Committee under command of Lt. Colonel Pollard from whom	
	1/6/15		Lt. Colonel H. A. Moore took over command from whom	
	28/9/15		Lt. Colonel (then Major) J. St. J. Atkinson took over command	
			Battalion first in billets at Leeds then at Ilkley, then in Hutments at Skipton	J.H.S
	1/6/15		Moved to Masham under canvas	
Chiseldon	28/8/15		Moved to Hutments at Chiseldon	J.H.S
Perham Down	23/11/15		Moved to No. 3 Camp Perham Down	J.H.S
Larkhill	2/12/15		Moved to No. 12 Camp Larkhill (Canada Lines)	J.H.S
Perham Down	18/12/15		Returned to No. 3 Camp.	J.H.S
Do.	24/1/16		Received orders to hold itself in readiness for embarkation.	J.H.S
Do.	26/1/16		Received orders for entraining en route for France. Captn. Rose left for Southampton.	J.H.S
Do.	31/1/16		Battalion entrained in 3 trains at full strength with machine guns (4 Lewis) and Transport complete	J.H.S List of Officers Appendix 1.
Southampton	31/1/16		Detrained and embarked at Southampton in 3 Detachments on Duchess of Argyll	J.H.S
Havre	1/2/16		Disembarked after smooth crossing. Marched to Camp at Harfleur. under canvas.	J.H.S
Do.	2/2/16		Inspected by Col. Clarke Inspector of Drafts.	J.H.S
Do.	2/2/16		Battalion (less Captn. Huffam and 105 men) marched to Havre with Transport and entrained at Gare des	J.H.S
		midnight	Marchandaises No. 3 Point	J.H.S
Blendeques	3/2/16		Detrained and marched to billets at Campagne arriving 4 a.m. Captn. Rose rejoined at BLENDEQUES	J.H.S

1875 Wt. W593/826 1,000,000 4/15 J.B.C. & A. A.D.S.S./Forms/C. 2118.

Instructions regarding War Diaries and Intelligence Summaries are contained in F. S. Regs., Part II. and the Staff Manual respectively. Title Pages will be prepared in manuscript.

Army Form C. 2118

WAR DIARY
or
INTELLIGENCE SUMMARY
(Erase heading not required.)

Place	Date	Hour	Summary of Events and Information	Remarks and references to Appendices
CAMPAGNE	4/2/16		Captn Huffam reported with his detachment of 105 men	J.H.S
C. Do	5/2/16		Interpreter [illegible] Lot. Mission Militaire Francaise. shared with 19th Durh. L. I reported for duty and attached for rations.	J.H.S
		11.30am	German aeroplane over billets chased by two of our aeroplanes and shelled. Very fine.	
Do	6/2/16		In billets.	
Do	7/2/16		Do Route march.	J.H.S
Do	8/2/16		Received orders to move tomorrow to billets in area BOESEGHEM - THIENNES. Captains Mason, Huffam, Crawford and Bell with 8 N.C.O.s and 4 officers batmen proceeded to LA GORGUE to report to Guards Division for instruction. 2/Lieut Braithwaite ordered to proceed to St VENANT tomorrow to attend mortar school.	J.H.S
	9/2/16	10.45 am	Marched from Campagne. Marched in Brigade by RACQUINGHEM - WITTES. & in WIDDEBROUCQ	J.H.S
BOESEGHEM	9/2/16	2 pm	BOESEGHEM. into billets. Inspected on march by Sir Douglas Haig and H.R.H. Prince Arthur of Connaught.	J.H.S
Do	10/2/16		In Billets	J.H.S
Do	11/2/16	11.15am	Inspected with Division by Field Marshall Lord Kitchener. Very wet.	J.H.S
Do	12/2/16		In billets - fine.	J.H.S
Do	13/2/16		In billets. Orders received "From midnight 13/14 Feby to midnight 17/18 Feby 35th Divn will be G.H.Q. reserve. Arrangements being made for transport by rail of Divn to other parts of British Zone. Hold ourselves in readiness to entrain at 8 hours notice or less."	J.H.S
Do	14/2/16		In billets. Route march. Captains Mason, Huffam, Crawford & Bell with 8 N.C.O.s and 4 officers batmen reported for duty on return from LA GORGUE	J.H.S
Do	15/2/16		In billets. Received arrangements for entrainment and detrainment of 35th Division in case a move by rail is ordered.	J.H.S
Do	16/2/16		In billets. All Officers attended Lecture by Lt Gen. Sir R.C.B. Haking K.C.B. Commanding XIth Army Corps - at Aire. Extract from London Gazette, Feb 12th 1916. W Yorks Regt - Temp. Capt. J.H. Gill to be temp: Major. 28/12/15. Temp: Lieut B.L. Wilcken to be temp: Capt. 28/12/15. Temporary 2nd Lieuts to be temporary Lieuts - F.J. Walker. 28/12/15. W.H. Colbeck. A.F. Hoggett. A.M. Hamilton, and E.C. Hardaker. 29/12/15. Information received from H.Q. 106th Brigade, that - "106th BDE Group will move to LES LAURIERS area (N.W of MERVILLE) on Feb: 19th. "On Feb: 20th 17th R Scots and 17th W Yorks will proceed for attachment to 19th Division."	E.C.
Do	17/2/16		In Billets. Route march. Orders received that - "The 106th Brigade Group will move into the Reserve Division billets of the XI Corps tomorrow. ... and will march via CROIX MARRAISSE - LE SART. Billets at LES LAURIERS and MERVILLE. Batt. Order 120. "Maj Gill will take over Command of W Coy from 6 p.m. 18th inst. Capt Crawford will be transferred to Y Coy. 2nd Lt Brown, Y Coy, to be acting Adjutant."	E.C.

1875 Wt. W593/826 1,000,000 4/15 J.B.C. & A. A.D.S.S./Forms/C. 2118.

Instructions regarding War Diaries and Intelligence Summaries are contained in F. S. Regs., Part II. and the Staff Manual respectively. Title Pages will be prepared in manuscript.

WAR DIARY
or
INTELLIGENCE SUMMARY
(Erase heading not required.)

Army Form C. 2118

Place	Date	Hour	Summary of Events and Information	Remarks and references to Appendices
MERVILLE.	18/2/16		Batt^n moved into the Reserve Division billets of the XIth Corps, 1st Army at MERVILLE. Maj: Gill took over command of W Coy. Capt: Crawford 2nd in Command of Y Coy. 2nd Lt Cross took over A/Adjutancy. Orders received at 11-20 p.m. that the "Battalion will move tomorrow, 19th inst, to billets at LE SART, North of the canal. E.C. . . . . will be clear of its present billets by 11-30 a.m."	
LE SART.	19/2/16		Batt^n moved into billets at LE SART. Instructions received for the attachment of the 35th Div: to the 19th and 38th Div^n for training in Trench Warfare. Brigade Message 11 p.m reported a Zeppelin moving N.W towards VEILLE CHAPELLE. E.C.	
W+Z Coys at RIEZ BAILLEUL and PONT DU HEM respectively. X+Y Coys in the trenches.	20/2/16		Batt^n marched off at 11-15 a.m. via MERVILLE, thence East to LA GORGUE. Halt at LA GORGUE for dinner, and to distribute Gas helmets. A short service was held in the concert room at 3-15 by the C of E chaplain. The Batt^n moved off at 4 o'c, guides from the 9th Welsh Regt, 9th Royal Welsh Fusiliers, 9th Cheshires + 6th Wilts having reported to take the several Companies to their respective billets or meeting places. W Coy marched into billets at RIEZ BAILLEUL and were attached to the 9th Cheshire Regt. X Coy were attached to the 9th Royal Welsh Fusiliers, and, accompanied by the C.O, Adj:^t M.O. and Signalling officer, went to the trenches with them, marching via FONT ROCHON and RIEZ BAILLEUL. Y Coy went to the trenches, being attached to the 9th Welsh Regt: and marching via LA BASSEE road. Z Coy, attached to the 6th Wiltshire Regt, marched into billets at PONT DU HEM via the LA BASSEE road. – The Batt^n Bombing and Machine Gun officers accompanied Y Coy and the 9th Welsh Regt., Bombers Signallers and Machine Gunners were divided equally amongst Coys. – The relief of the two Coys going into the trenches was completed by 9 p.m. At 10-45 the first casualty in the Batt^n took place, Pte Catton, X Coy, being shot through the head by bullets from a German Machine Gun which traversed the parapet. Gas attack expected, but did not take place. The part of the trenches held by the 9th RWF and the 9th Welsh Regt. was the sector N.E of NEUVE CHAPELLE, and opposite the AUBERS RIDGE. Quarter Master attached to the 9th Cheshire depot. Transport returned to billets at LE SART. Weather clear. E.C.	
DO.	21/2/16		Artillery activity on both sides during the forenoon and afternoon, – our own artillery being more active than the German. – A severe Bombardment of the German parapet by trench Mortars was carried out by the 9th R.W.F^s about mid-day. Violent cannonade heard in Southerly direction, afterwards found to be at LOOS. Weather clear. E.C.	
W+Z Coys took the place of X+Y Coys, + Vice Versa.	22/2/16		Rain in the morning, which turned to snow. Very cold. The 9th Cheshires, accompanied by W Coy, relieved the 9th RWF^s and X Coy. The 6th Wiltshires, accompanied by Z Coy, relieved the 9th Welsh Regt. and Y Coy. The 2nd in Command was attached to the 6th Wiltshire Regt. X+Y Coys marched to billets at RIEZ BAILLEUL and PONT DU HEM respectively. Orders received for changes in attachment, to take place on the 24th. E.C.	
W+Z Coys in trenches. X+Y in billets at RIEZ BAILLEUL and PONT DU HEM.	23/2/16		Snow continued to fall. Very cold. Roads bad. 1 Casualty in W Coy. – Killed. E.C.	
RIEZ BAILLEUL. PONT DU HEM. + trenches.	24/2/16		W+Z Coys came out of the trenches and were attached in billets at RIEZ BAILLEUL and PONT DU HEM. to the 8th N. Staffs Regt: and the 10th Royal Warwickshire Regt: respectively. X+Y Coys were attached respectively to the 7th Gloucester Regt, and the 10th Worcestershire Regt, and went into the trenches with them. Casualties – 1 other rank wounded, W Coy. – Snow, + weather very cold. C.O. Adj: M.O. + Signalling officer attached to 8th N. Staffs Regt. 2nd in Command, Machine Gun + Bombing officers, with Batt^n Sgt Major attached to the 10th Royal Warwickshire Regt. E.C.	

1875 Wt. W593/826 1,000,000 4/15 J.B.C. & A. A.D.S.S./Forms/C. 2118.

Appendix 1. War Diary

17th (S) Battalion. West Yorkshire Regiment.

Lieut. Col.

F. St. J. Atkinson.

Major.

P. S. Hall.

Captains.

Mason. G. H.
Huffam. S.
Crawford. A. B.
Bell. S. L.
Rose. J. A. (Embarkation Officer)
Hadow. E. G.

Lieutenants.

Wilcher. B. L.
Cohen. A. B.
Banks. C. W.
Fricker. E.
Hepper. E. R.

2nd. Lieutenants.

Hoggett. A. B.
Hamilton. A. M.
Hardaker. E. C.
Colbeck. W. H.
Braithwaite. A. N.
Stead. W. W.
Sutherland. G. A.
de Witt. C. A.
Tadman. A. S.
Hitchen. S. L.
Cross. E.
Westcott. A. B.
Lachlan. C. G.
Walker. F. T.
Marshall. H. W. H.
Redman. W.
Wootton. J. N.

Adjutant:- Capt. J. H. Gill.

Quartermaster:- Lieut. P. Valette.

Medical Officer:- Lieut. E. A. Wilson. (R.A.M.C. attached).

2nd. Lt. H. A. Schaap. left behind as O.C. Details.

C O N F I D E N T I A L.

W A R D I A R Y

OF

17TH (S) BATTN. WEST YORKSHIRE REGIMENT.

From 1st March 1916 To 31st March 1916.

V O L U M E 2.

17 W Yorks
Vol 2

35

Army Form C. 2118

Instructions regarding War Diaries and Intelligence Summaries are contained in F. S. Regs., Part II. and the Staff Manual respectively. Title Pages will be prepared in manuscript.

WAR DIARY
or
INTELLIGENCE SUMMARY
(Erase heading not required.)

Place	Date	Hour	Summary of Events and Information	Remarks and references to Appendices
LE SART.	1/3/16		Orders received that the Battn will move to LA GORGUE tomorrow and be attached to the 19th Division. Day spent in billets. Lectures by C.O. to 2nd Lts and N.C.O's. weather fine. E.C.	
LE SART and LA GORGUE	2/3/16		The Battn moved to LA GORGUE. Parade – 10-30 a.m. Arrived in LA GORGUE at 12-10. All settled into billets at once. weather fine. E.C.	
LA GORGUE	3/3/16		5 Officers and 260 men went as Working Parties to RE at Epinette farm, M.16.d. Rest of Battn at work in billets. 5 Officers and 250 men went to the same place at 4-30 p.m. A very wet day. E.C.	
Do.	4/3/16.		2 Officers + 75 men went as working party to L'EPINETTE farm. Another party arranged for the afternoon was cancelled. Bathing at 19th DIVISIONAL baths at LA GORGUE for Z Coy + some of Y Coy and HQrs unit. A wet + cold day. E.C.	
Do.	5/3/16.		Church Parade at 9-20. Baths for W Coy and HQrs unit at LESTREM. Working party 2 Officers + 45 men went to EPINETTE farm. Working party of 2 Officers + 100 men at Epinette at night. E.C.	
Do.	6/3/16.		Orders received for taking over part of the line by 106th BDE under attachment to 19th Division. Two working parties, 2 Officers + 45 men, and 1 Officer and 50 men went to EPINETTE farm. Lecture by C.O. to Officers at 5-30. "Trench standing orders" published for the Battalion. A cold wet day with some snow. E.C.	
LA GORGUE and Trenches	7/3/16.		The Battn relieved the 10th Royal Warwickshire Regt in the trenches, taking over from ERITH STREET M.24.2. to MIN. STREET M.29.3. 5 Posts also taken over – N. Keeley Post, Dreadnought Post, Erith Post, Grants Post, and Winchester Post. W Coy in the Posts. Z Coy the Rt Coy in the line. Y Coy centre Coy. X Coy Left Coy. Relief complete by 9-30 p.m. 2nd West Yorks on our left. Battn on our right – 17th Royal Scots. Night passed quietly. Snow on the ground, and today was very cold – work on fire step and pumping during the night. E.C.	
Trenches. M.24.2.– M.29.3.	8/3/16.		Our artillery active, knocked enemy parapet about opposite M.30.2. – another bombardment in the evening opposite the "Bird Cage" M.30.1. Enemy retaliated 3 times during the day on ERITH POST. We retaliated for ERITH effectively, + got retaliation in 3 minutes on the last occasion. – Our parapet breached in one place. Wire to ERITH cut on 3rd time of shelling, but communication established again at once. Much subsidence of Parapet + traverses due to frost + thaw. Tree man-handled (?). Day cold. E.C.	
Do.	9/3/16.		Our artillery bombarded enemy from 10-20 a.m. – 12 noon. 300 Shrapnel fired. Breach made in their parapet by our artillery. Working party of Germans on extreme left stopped by our Snipers while repairing. Enemy knocked in our parapet at M.30.1. [illegible] Erith Post again shelled & retaliation called for. – Shells fell 50 yds in rear of M.30.1 about 11.40 a.m. 3 Patrols went out at night, one from each Coy. 1 Officer + 3 men from Rt. and Centre Coy, 1 Officer + 4 men from Left Coy. – Patrol from Rt Coy discovered an enemy Machine Gun firing over parapet in Crater 34. Not much information owing to darkness. weather, cold & wet, sleet and snow at times. E.C.	

1879 Wt. W593/826 1,000,000 4/15 J.B.C. & A. A.D.S.S./Forms/C. 2118.

Instructions regarding War Diaries and Intelligence Summaries are contained in F. S. Regs., Part II. and the Staff Manual respectively. Title Pages will be prepared in manuscript.

WAR DIARY
or
INTELLIGENCE SUMMARY

(Erase heading not required.)

Army Form C. 2118

Place	Date	Hour	Summary of Events and Information	Remarks and references to Appendices
~~10/3/16.~~ Trenches M.24.2 — M.29.3	10/3/16.	1·30p.m 2·30p.m	Bombardment of enemy front line. Centre Coy cleared to flanks by arrangement. Direct hits on enemy parapet at M.30.c.5.6. Wire cut at M.24.d.5.2. Our Lewis Guns fired on breaches made at night. Lewis Guns paid special attention to Crater 34. Working party dispersed at M.30.c.5.1. about dusk. ERITH POST again shelled twice by enemy, retaliation called for. N Tilleloy also shelled, but little damage was done. Patrol went out from the Rt Coy from 9·30–11·10p.m. Fired on by M.G. from Crater 34. A Patrol from Left Coy gained no information. — Intelligence Officer learned that Crater 34 almost certainly is linked up with enemy front line, and a M.G. brought along tunnel at night. Working parties provided for R.E. — 2 men wearing steel helmets in ERITH POST both had them dented. They were the only 2 wearing them, tho only 2 hit. E.C.	
Do and PONT DU HEM.	11/3/16.		Battn relieved by 19th D.L.I. & moved back to billets at PONT DU HEM. Relief worked smoothly & was completed by 9 p.m. 2 men wounded during the day and LIEUT. BANKS was touched in the leg during the Relief. We took over MIN and LONELY Posts from D.L.I. and relieved their LEWIS Gun in Winchester Post. E.C.	
PONT DU HEM.	12/3/16		Baths for most of the men of Y & Z Coys at PONT RIQUEUL. Battn now in Brigade reserve, and preparations made for duties in case Battn called on. X Coy relieved men of W in MIN and LONELY Posts. E.C.	
Do.	13/3/16		Working Parties provided all day for R.E. to the number of 9 Officers and 350 men. Bathing continued at PONT RIQUEUL. Orders received that the Battn will move to PARADIS tomorrow. E.C.	
Do and Paradis.	14/3/16		10th Worcestershire Regt. relieved the Battn in the billets at PONT DU HEM. Battn marched to billets at PARADIS in the CALONNE area. (Q.18 & 24 on BETHUNE combined sheet) Paraded at 10·30 arrived 1·30–2·0 c. Marched by Coys according to orders, at 300 yds intervals. All settled in very quickly. A beautiful clear day. Sunshine. Roads in good condition. E.C.	
PARADIS.	15/3/16.		Day spent quietly in billets in cleaning up. Meeting of Officers at 5·30. Gas alarm at 11p.m. Battalion was turned out & stood to arms. Alarm over in a few minutes. A beautiful clear day. Roads good. E.C.	
Do.	16/3/16.		Route march via Q.23c. Q.16d. Q.9b. Q.4c. Q.5b. Paradis. — Rest of day in billets. Weather good & roads good. E.C.	
Do.	17/3/16	—	Day spent in billets — employed in bombing, wiring etc. E.C.	
Do	18/3/16.		Brigade Canteen opened at Paradis. Q.24.c.9.7. — Day spent in billets. Orders received for move to LE SART tomorrow 19/3/16. Capt Rose, billeting officer, went to make arrangements. Decided that the Battn will billet at MERVILLE, as 35th Divisional Cyclists have occupied billets at LE SART. E.C.	

1875 Wt. W593/826 1,000,000 4/15 J.B.C. & A. A.D.S.S./Forms/C. 2118.

Instructions regarding War Diaries and Intelligence Summaries are contained in F. S. Regs., Part II. and the Staff Manual respectively. Title Pages will be prepared in manuscript.

WAR DIARY
or
INTELLIGENCE SUMMARY
(Erase heading not required.)

Army Form C. 2118

Place	Date	Hour	Summary of Events and Information	Remarks and references to Appendices
PARADIS and MERVILLE.	19/3/16.		Battn moved to MERVILLE. Billets at K21d. K22c.d. K28c. The C.O. 2nd in Command, C.C. Coys, Lewis Gun + Intelligence Officers went to visit the new line of trenches. – Move over by 12 noon, + all settled in, except X Coy + 2 Platoons Y Coy, who went as a Working Party to MESPLAUX. X14b. X15b. X8b. – Day clear roads good. E.L.	
MERVILLE	20/3/16		Baths for 240 men at CALONNE. The men were paid. Day spent in wiring, bombing etc. E.L.	
Do.	21/3/16		Working Parties at MESPLAUX – X14b – X15b, X8b – + CARTER'S POST K29c97. Baths for 320 men at CALONNE. Orders received that Battn will move on 24th + 25th. E.L.	
Do.	22/3/16		Parade for Roman Catholics, Service Merville Church at 7a.m. A working party went to CARTERS POST. Orders for move on 24th + 25th, and orders as to new line trenches, cancelled. E.L.	
Do	23/3/16		Day spent in billets. Weather holding good. The Commanding Officer visited new line of trenches. E.L.	
Do	24/3/16		Day spent in billets. Snow fell. Weather bad. Orders for move on 26/3/16. E.L.	
Do	25/3/16.		2nd in Command, C.C. Coys. Lewis Gun Officer, Intelligence Officer, Signalling Officer, Bombing Officer, Transport Officer, and Sniping Officer visited new line of trenches. Transport for tomorrow's move reported at 6 p.m. Billets to be at NEUF BERQUIN.	
Do and NEUF BERQUIN.	26/3/16.		The Battn moved to billets at NEUF BERQUIN. Parade at 2-30. Settled in billets by 4-30. Rain. M.3.c.33. (Sheet-36) E.L.	
NEUF BERQUIN and Trenches.	27/3/16		The Battn took over Left Subsector of PETILLON Sector of the line. HQrs Eaton Hall, Line – N10.1. to N10.5 inclusive. Relief complete by 10-30 p.m. – Battn marched from NEUF BERQUIN via ESTAIRES SAILLY and BAC ST MAUR – weather very bad. Rain and sleet. A most trying march for the men, who nevertheless worked well afterwards. Situation during the night – Normal. Pumping and raising of firing step was chief work of night. – E.L.	
Trenches. [PETILLON].	28/3/16		Snipers claimed a victim. Work by enemy observed wire going on at the Tadpole. – Patrols out but report too much water for anything effective to be done. Much work at traverses and parapet, which were not bullet proof, and low in places. E.L.	
Do.	29/3/16		4 Lewis Guns put in battle emplacements. 2 used as moveable guns. – Some interchange of Rifle Grenades. Unfortunate accident with rifle Grenade by which 1 man killed and 2 wounded. Some shelling by enemy of Cellar Farm and DEE Post. Patrol went out from Left Coy (Z Coy) water too deep to allow of useful information being gained. Snipers very active all along the front. They have a loophole in nearly every bay, + their position from where firing is thus difficult to locate. Night passed quietly. Much work done. E.L.	

Army Form C. 2118

Instructions regarding War Diaries and Intelligence Summaries are contained in F. S. Regs., Part II. and the Staff Manual respectively. Title Pages will be prepared in manuscript.

WAR DIARY

~~or~~

~~INTELLIGENCE SUMMARY~~

(Erase heading not required.)

Place	Date	Hour	Summary of Events and Information	Remarks and references to Appendices
RIEZ BAILLEUL, PONT DU HEM. and Trenches.	25/2/16.		X and Y Coys in the trenches, attached to the 8th Gloucestershire Regt and the 10th Worcestershire Regt respectively. W and Z Coys in billets at RIEZ BAILLEUL and PONT DU HEM respectively, attached to the 8th N STAFFS REGT and the 10th ROYAL WARWICKSHIRE Regt. - More snow fell, and Coys were issued with sheep skin coats and waterproof capes. Orders received that W+Z Coys would go into trenches for one night on the night of 26/2/16, with the Regts to which they are attached in billets at present. - Roads bad owing to snow and frost.	E.P.
Do.	26/2/16.		Orders received on 25/2/16 carried out. W Coy went into trenches with the 8th North Staffs Regt, the 2nd in Command + Z Coy with the 10th Royal Warwickshire Regt. X and Y Coys came out of the trenches and occupied the billets vacated by W and Z Coys respectively.	E.P.
Trenches LE SART.	27/2/16.		The C.O Adjt, X and Y Coys marched back to billets at LE SART. Parade at 10-30, and all were in billets by 1-30. W and Z Coys came out of the trenches, and occupied the billets vacated by X and Y Coys. A clear day and a thaw set in. Roads bad.	E.P.
LE SART.	28/2/16		X and Y Coys went to baths at St VENANT. much appreciated: W and Z Coys marched from RIEZ BAILLEUL to billets at LE SART. The battalion linked up once more.	E.P.
Do	29/2/16		W, X and Y Coys had parties of 40 men on fatigue at the Forest of NIEPPE Rifle Range, W and Z Coys on fatigue at the coal dump, MERVILLE. - Conference of officers at HQ LE SART, when the experiences of the previous week were discussed, and decisions as to future action arrived at.	E.P.

Army Form C. 2118

Instructions regarding War Diaries and Intelligence Summaries are contained in F. S. Regs., Part II. and the Staff Manual respectively. Title Pages will be prepared in manuscript.

WAR DIARY
or
INTELLIGENCE SUMMARY
(Erase heading not required.)

Place	Date	Hour	Summary of Events and Information	Remarks and references to Appendices
Trenches.	30/3/16.		Snipers kept under by left Coy and left centre Coy (Z and Y Coys respectively) Still active on the right opposite W (Right Coy) and X (Right Centre) Coy. Snipers claim 3 victims. - Trench Mortar started to work in our lines. Drew retaliation with trench mortars and Rifle Grenades. Lewis Guns did much useful work during the night and claim at least 1 victim of a party seen at 5 a.m. - Party seen wearing caps of light blue colour with white bands and blue or Red badges, at Div: Post G2. Snipers opened on them. Much work done on parapets & parados. Night passed without any serious incident. Weather good. Sunshine & dry. [initials]	
Do and FLEURBAIX	31/3/16		Day passed quietly. - Relieved at night by 19th DLI. Relief complete by 9-30 p.m. Battn went into billets and posts in and around FLEURBAIX. - MAJOR G. ILL wounded by a Rifle Grenade. Not seriously. Weather good [initials]	

1875 Wt. W593/826 1,000,000 4/15 J.B.C. & A. A.D.S.S./Forms/C. 2118.

CONFIDENTIAL

W A R D I A R Y

OF

17TH (S) BN WEST YORKSHIRE REGIMENT.

From 1st April 1916 to 30th April 1916

VOLUME 3.

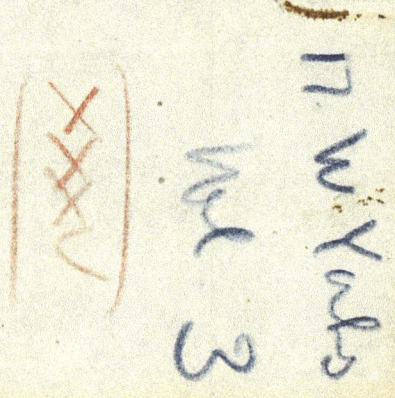

WAR DIARY
or
INTELLIGENCE SUMMARY

(Erase heading not required.)

Army Form C. 2118.

Instructions regarding War Diaries and Intelligence Summaries are contained in F. S. Regs., Part II. and the Staff Manual respectively. Title Pages will be prepared in manuscript.

Place	Date	Hour	Summary of Events and Information	Remarks and references to Appendices
FLEURBAIX.	1/4/16.		In billets. W and Z Coys in Posts at CROIX BLANCHE and RUE DE QUESNES. Z Coy heavily shelled, but little damage done. Weather and roads very good. E.C.	
Do.	2/4/16		Posts + billets. Coy Church Parades in the morning. Weather good, and day quiet. E.C.	
Do.	3/4/16.		Do – Military Cross awarded to 2nd Lt YORKE 18th H.L.I. 106th Bde, for work at DUCKS BILL after mine explosion. Weather + roads still good. E.C.	
Do and NEUF BERQUIN	4/4/16.		106th Bde relieved in PETILLON Sector by 104th Bde. Relief complete by 7-30 a.m. the place of 17th West Yorks being taken by 18th Lancashire Fusiliers. Battalion marched by Coys to NEUF BERQUIN and settled in by 10-30 a.m. Weather and roads very good. E.C.	
NEUF BERQUIN.	5/4/16.		In billets. Baths at SAILLY. Day spent in rest and cleaning up. Capt CRAWFORD took over command of W Coy in absence of MAJOR GILL, wounded. Weather + roads good. E.C.	
Do.	6/4/16.		Brigade Courses in TRENCH MORTAR and SNIPING commenced. – G.O.C. 35th DIVISION inspected the Battalion and was satisfied with work done hitherto. Day spent in billets. Weather + roads very good. E.C.	
Do and ESTAIRES.	7/4/16.	2-30 pm	Battn moved to billets at ESTAIRES during the afternoon. – Billets found to be in a very dirty condition. Settled in by 4 p.m. Roads + weather good. E.C.	
ESTAIRES	8/4/16.		Training under Coy arrangements. Roads + weather good. E.C.	
Do	9/4/16.		Church Parade 11 a.m. R.C.s at 10.30 a.m. Voluntary services – C of E. 8 a.m. Nonconformists at 2-30 + 6-30 p.m. Lecture by C.O. to officers at 12 noon. Weather + roads very good. E.C.	
Do	10/4/16.		Brigadier General Carey took over command of 35th Div during absence on leave of Major General Pinney. C.O visited new line – FAUQUISSART Section. Orders received for move and relief on 12/4/16. Battn to relieve 14th GLOUCESTER REGT. Weather good. E.C.	
Do.	11/4/16.		Bathed at SAILLY for 80 men. Lecture by C.O to Officers at 12 noon. 1 Officer per Coy, Platoon Sergeants, Snipers, and a Patrol party from each Coy went to trenches to take over. Weather changing. Some rain. E.C.	
Do and Trenches. N.13.6 – N.8.2.	12/4/16		Battn relieved 14th Gloucestershire Regt in FAUQUISSART SECTION. – Left Subsector: W Coy on Right – N.13.6. N.13.7. X Coy. Rt Centre. N.14.1. Y Coy. Left Centre. N.8.1. Left Coy. Z Coy. – N.8.2. Relief complete by 9-35 p.m. Night passed quietly. One man wounded + Lewis Gun disabled. Patrols were out to examine our wire. – Much work done – Weather bad. Rain. E.C.	
Do	13/4/16		Enemy fired Rifle Grenades + T.M.s without doing any damage. Snipers active and 1 N.C.O. killed. Some retaliation with rifle Grenades on the Right with good effect. Shelling of Rue Tilleloy + Rotten Row. C. French.	

2449 Wt. W14957/M90 750,000 1/16 J.B.C. & A. Forms/C.2118/12.

Army Form C. 2118.

WAR DIARY
or
INTELLIGENCE SUMMARY

(Erase heading not required.)

Instructions regarding War Diaries and Intelligence Summaries are contained in F. S. Regs., Part II. and the Staff Manual respectively. Title Pages will be prepared in manuscript.

Place	Date	Hour	Summary of Events and Information	Remarks and references to Appendices
13/4 Trenches	13/4/16 contd.		Patrols from all 4 Coys. No mans land reported in good condition. Our wire reported weak. Moon too bright to allow of much information being gained. Left Coy discovered a beam pile which will be made into a listening post. Work on parapets & parados, drainage etc.	E.P.
DO.	14/4/16		German line enfiladed by Lewis Gun from Red Lamp Salient, N.13.6. Power cables observed & cut by Th gun fire. Retaliation by artillery for shelling of our trenches in reserve line. Snipers claim 3 victims. Pigeons seen going to and from German line, in and from direction of PONT DU HEM. Light seen at houses 170° Magnetic & 120° Magnetic variation from Hauk Post. A Gun flash seen at 170° from Hauk Post. Also a party carrying boxes. Patrols out from Rt Coy & Left Centre Coy. German line seems to be thinly held. No mans land in good condition. Night passed quietly. Weather fair.	E.P.
Do and ESTAIRES.	15/4/16		Battn relieved by 10th S.W.B. Relief complete without incident by 9-30 p.m. Battn marched by Coys to billets at ESTAIRES. Into billets by 11-30 pm.	E.P.
ESTAIRES and CROIX BARBÉE	16/4/16		Battn paraded at 9 a.m. marched to reserve billets at CROIX BARBÉE. M.26.c.7.3. 5 Posts manned and relief of billets complete by 12 noon. Posts manned by Y Coy. - EUSTON. M.34.a.1.8. Loretto. M.33.b.2.5. Sheet 36. Care taking garrisons in Vieille Chapelle R.28.d.6.6. 4 men, Wellington R.29.d.2.9. Huit Maison S. R.29.b.9.5. Sheet 36.a. Some shelling of billets but no damage. Weather very good.	E.P.
CROIX BARBÉE	17/4/16		Day spent in billets. Passed quietly. Weather showery & changeable. Rather cold.	E.P.
DO.	18/4/16		Day in billets. Weather good. Some shelling	E.B.
Do	19/4/16		Battn at Croix Barbée. Garrison of 3 caretaking Posts named 16/4/16 were relieved by men unfit for trench work. Some shelling. Weather good.	E.P.
Do and Trenches	20/4/16		The Battn relieved the 19th D.L.I. in left Subsector, NEUVE CHAPELLE Section. Relief complete 10 p.m. W Coy Left. M.35.1. M.35.2. Sheet Area I. Z Coy Rt. S.5.3. S.5.4. Y Coy centre S.5.5. S.5.6. W Coy hold Chateau Post - Z Coy Church Post in addition to front line. X Coy in Moggs Hole, B line, Curzon Post. Retaliation for Rifle Grenades. Lewis Guns fired on Sniper at night. Snipers claim 2 certain hits. Also on an M.G. at M.35.d.7.8. which was silenced. Brewery shelled and silenced them. Also 4 direct hits on our parapet at S.5.5 & S.5.6 at 4 p.m. Working party seen at S.5.b.6.3. Uniforms of dark grey. Men seen pushing trolley opposite the Brewery. Two shots fired & work ceased! Pigeons seen going to German line. - Snipers put in 3 new loopholes. Much work on drains, parapets, parados, traverses.	E.P.

2449 Wt. W14957/M90 750,000 1/16 J.B.C. & A. Forms/C.2118/12.

Army Form C. 2118.

Instructions regarding War Diaries and Intelligence Summaries are contained in F. S. Regs., Part II. and the Staff Manual respectively. Title Pages will be prepared in manuscript.

WAR DIARY
or
INTELLIGENCE SUMMARY
(Erase heading not required.)

Place	Date	Hour	Summary of Events and Information	Remarks and references to Appendices
Trenches S5.3. S5.4. S5.5. S5.6. M35.1. M35.2. Area 1.	21/4/16.		Snipers claim 1 victim. Combined operation between Artillery, Trench Mortars, H.T.M.G.'s at 5 p.m. Lewis Guns in front line joined in. Enemy retaliated with 4.2" and Shrapnel. No damage done. Enemy had a very fast M.G. firing at S.5.b.8.0. Patrols out report our wire weak. Enemy line weakly held. Wiring party seen at 3-10 a.m. Flashlight observed at intervals, which had been seen previous night. Enemy sent up many lights. Working party seen at S.5.b.6.4. Another one at N corner of Rue du Bois carrying planks. Much activity at this point. S.6.a.6.4. Enemy M.G. located at S.5.d.6.3. when firing at an aeroplane. Much work done. Sandbags filled. Parapets, parados, traverses, strengthened and heightened. Duck boards renewed. Twired work on Officers' dug out. Snipers put 4 loop holes in use. F.P.	
DO	22/4/16		Sniper located at M.35.d.9.3. Fired at twice after that the loophole remained closed. Artillery activity. Enemy more active with M.G.s than previous nights. Day hazy + cloudy, observation difficult. Pumping was observed at S.5.b.5.2. Four shots fired from Brewery on a trolley pushed by 4 or 5 Germans. No results observed owing to bad light. Parties were seen coming out of house at N W corner of Rue du Bois. Officers patrol went out opposite S.5.b.4.3. + got within 20x of enemy parapet. Patrol retired on appearance of a strong enemy patrol. Lewis Guns opened fire with unknown results. Flashlight again seen at S.5.b.7.7½. Work on Church Rd. C. Trench wiring. 3 Listening Posts put out in front of our wire, one in a cart – all put in use. Snipers opened 2 more loopholes. Now 13 in the line in use, as against 8 taken over, 5 of which were not useable. F.P.	
Do.	23/4/16.		Trench Mortar fired on M.35.2. Enemy retaliated with H.E. and Shrapnel. M.G.s traversed enemy wire + parapet, Rue du Bois road in front of it. Much aeroplane activity. Germans seen issuing from house at S.6.a.6.4. Man wearing dark round cap with light blue band appeared of our parapet. He was fired at and disappeared. To left of Fish Back S.5.d.8½.5. is a wheel similar to those used for dogs. A trolley line runs behind up to Fish Back where it stops. Germans seen pushing a trolley. They wore grey jerseys and round hats. Enemy seen to be strengthening 2nd line by the Bois. Water pumped from salient opposite the N.E.B. Mining appears to be taking place here as earth thrown up is dark green when wet, and lightish grey when dry. Only just begun. A building near S.5.d.6.3. is obviously used for storage as trolley stops there + boxes carried in. Officers caps seen at 11 a.m. Gold braid on them. Accompanying the Officers was a bayonet man whose bayonet showed as he walked. Pigeon flew from Rue du Bois. Two O.P.s in Rue du Bois were located. A Sniper or observer seen climbing up to one of them which was shielded with iron plates.	

2449 Wt. W14957/M90 750,000 1/16 J.B.C. & A. Forms/C.2118/12.

Instructions regarding War Diaries and Intelligence Summaries are contained in F. S. Regs., Part II. and the Staff Manual respectively. Title Pages will be prepared in manuscript.

Army Form C. 2118

WAR DIARY
or
INTELLIGENCE SUMMARY

(Erase heading not required.)

Place	Date	Hour	Summary of Events and Information	Remarks and references to Appendices
			3 M bombs (unexploded) were discovered in the N.E.B. Detonators appear to have been taken out. One bomb still smoking, having spontaneously combusted. - A German seen in a hollow in No Mans Land at 5.30 pm wore a chocolate coloured round peakless cap with broad white band & a light blue tunic. 2 Rifle Grenades were fired at him. He dug himself in. Upper patrol, 19th D.L.I. reports wire of enemy strong & thick. - a sniper's loophole put in at M35.1. A Lewis Gun night emplacement completed in M35.2. Wiring, filling sandbags, work on parapets, fire steps etc.	E.P.
Do and Croix Barbée	24/4/16	9-35 p.m	Battn was relieved by 19th DLI and returned to billets at Croix Barbée. Relief complete. A quiet day, much aeroplane activity. X Coy held Euston and Lorette Posts with 2 Platoons after the relief. Colonel ATKINSON went on leave. An alarm at night - which came to nothing.	E.P.
Croix Barbée	25/4/16		A quiet day in billets. Day clear and fine. Working parties provided.	E.P.
	26/4/16		Day spent quietly in billets. Working parties provided.	E.P.
Do.	27/4/16		Baths at Croix Barbée. Working parties.	
Do	28/4/16		Battn moved to Billets at Les Lobes being relieved by 18th Lancashire Fusiliers of 104th Bde which took over the NEUVE CHAPELLE Section. Working parties in the morning. Relief began at 5 p.m. Lt COHEN wounded with Shrapnel at Croix Barbée during relief.	E.P.
Do and Les Lobes	29/4/16		Training in billets. Weather very good.	E.P.
	30/4/16		Working parties. ~~Church~~ Parade Services for men of all denominations. Weather good.	E.P.

C O N F I D E N T I A L.

W A R   D I A R Y

-- of --

17TH (S) BATTN. WEST YORKSHIRE REGT.,

From 1st June 1916 To 30th June 1916.

VOLUME V.

......xxxxxxxxx......

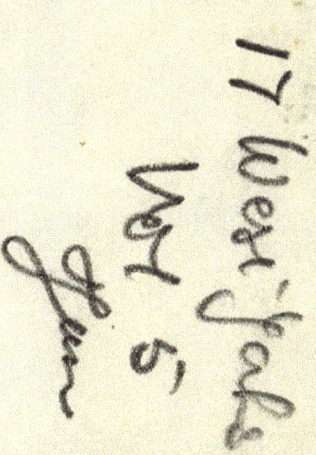

Instructions regarding War Diaries and Intelligence Summaries are contained in F. S. Regs., Part II. and the Staff Manual respectively. Title Pages will be prepared in manuscript.

WAR DIARY
or
INTELLIGENCE SUMMARY
(Erase heading not required.)

Army Form C. 2118

Place	Date	Hour	Summary of Events and Information	Remarks and references to Appendices
Trenches. Festubert	1/6/16		The Battn was relieved in the left sub section, Festubert Section, by 19th D.L.I. and marched to billets at LE TOURET. Relief complete 12-10 a.m. without incident. B Coy 2/4 Gloster Regt attached to the Battn for 8 days instruction.	E.C.
	2/6/16		Quiet day spent in billets. Weather good.	E.C.
	3/6/16		Notice received of award of Military Medal to 11694 L/Cpl C Rochett. 106 M.G. Coy. - Baths at Le Touret. Working parties numbering 370 men supplied to R.E. weather holding good. Roads good.	E.C.
	4/6/16		Parade Services for men of all denominations. Baths at Le Touret. Working parties numbering 500 men supplied to R.E. Lewis Gunners, Signallers + Snipers relieved those of D.L.I. in the line in front of O.B.L.	
	5/6/16		Battn relieved 19th D.L.I. in left subsection Festubert Section. Relief complete 11-10 p.m. W Coy left line Coy. Y Coy Rt line Coy. Z Coy Left Support Coy in O.B.L. X Coy Rt Support Coy in O.B.L. 3 Rifle Grenades fell near island 30 and 1 hit island 14 about 1 a.m. Lights were sent up by the enemy at the same time. Enemy M.G.s active. Snipers claim 1 victim at S22.c.6.1. Officers patrol from island 30A had to return owing to heavy M.G. fire. 5 patrols out in all. Wire in front of islands 16-24 reported fairly strong. In front of 24-26 weak. Front end of Shetland Rd was cleared. Fire steps heightened in O.B.L. Snipers loop hole plates put in in left and right cover trenches.	
	6/6/16		Whizz bangs fell near left cover trench about 5 p.m. and near island 27. We retaliated with Stokes gun. 30 more fell near Shetland Rd at about 6 p.m. + 2 near islands 34-38. We again retaliated with Stokes gun. 2 Salvoes Shrapnel burst over Indian village 2-30 p.m. Enemy M.G.s very active at night. 2nd LT B.L. HITCHEN was killed. Snipers claim 2 victims. 2 Enemy periscopes broken. Enemy patrol of about 10 men reported in front of island 29. Fire was opened, & patrol went out, but enemy patrol could not be found. Much work heard in progress in enemy line. Patrol out 9-30-12-30 watching ditch running from island 30 to German line. Has nothing to report. A red white & blue flag has been hoisted in No Mans Land S27.d.6.6. Men seen seem all either very young or about 45 and over. Enemy exposing himself more than formerly. Caps are various some black, green, grey, light blue, peaked and peakless. A telegraph wire reported, which runs over hill in the distance towards VIOLAINES about S.8 central. 2 posts can be seen upright thus. Parapet repaired. Snipers plates let in. Much wiring done. Work on Cr trenches between islands. Fire steps raised. New emplacement built for Stokes Gun. In O.B.L work on dugout at S26.b.4.0. Gaps made in the wire.	E.C.

1875 Wt. W593/826 1,000,000 4/15 J.B.C. & A. A.D.S.S./Forms/C. 2118.

Army Form C. 2118

Instructions regarding War Diaries and Intelligence Summaries are contained in F. S. Regs., Part II. and the Staff Manual respectively. Title Pages will be prepared in manuscript.

WAR DIARY
or
INTELLIGENCE SUMMARY

(Erase heading not required.)

Place	Date	Hour	Summary of Events and Information	Remarks and references to Appendices
Trenches. FESTUBERT Left Sub section	7/6/16		Enemy shelled left cover trench with Whizz Bangs from 7-30 a.m. intermittently. The parapet was slightly damaged but most fell short. One 4.2 hit the parapet. Retaliation called for 10-20, enemy silenced by 10-50 a.m. Shrapnel over Indian village 7-45 a.m. Snipers claim 2 victims at S22.c.6.1. and S28a.4.4. One enemy periscope broken. A man seen in mound at S28.a.4.6. pointing towards the position of Stokes Gun. Soon after several whizz bangs fell round it. It was removed to another emplacement. A covered "Comm" trench seen at S.28.c.3.6. down which a number of men passed during the day. Officer + 9 men went to investigate flag at S27.d.6.6. in No Mans Land. A rope was attached to the stick. The party retired & pulled the other end of the rope, whereupon a bomb attached to flag exploded. The flag was brought back. A M.G. was covering the spot. Officers patrol out to reconnoitre mound at S28.a.4.6 found no enemy or signs of enemy occupation. - Work - Parapet & parados strengthened in island 29. Damaged parapet repaired in island 31. S28.a.3.8. 40' of Parados commenced in islands 36-38. 40' also put up in Left cover trench (parados) Parapet repaired after shelling. Much wiring done. 40' parados built with hurdles & loose earth in Richmond Terrace. Dug out at S26 b.4.0 almost completed. Sandbags filled & fire steps raised - Loopholes for Observers let in to parapet in O.B.L - E.P.	
Do	8/6/16		Artillery activity on left 9-10 p.m. Enemy fired 15 rounds Shrapnel over Brewery about 9-15 a.m. Covered C" trench at S.28 c.3.7. much used again. 2 bee hives have been placed on enemy parados at S22 c.6.1. possibly have loop holes in. There is a M.G. in an old building at this point. Officers patrol reconnoitred our wire. Officers patrol out to watch suspected post at S28.a.4.6. It was not being used. 30x of wire put out in front of island 29. Parapet strengthened island 38. Parados built, islands 34.37 Left Cover trench. Reclaiming of trench on left of right cover trench. 7 bays cleared & others partially. O.B.L. work on Parados. 9 gaps made in wire in front. E.P.	
Do-	9/6/16		10-15 a.m. enemy fired whizz bangs over party working behind island 37. No damage done. 4 L.H.V shells fell in rear of cover trench. 3-25 p.m. Enemy snipers active on new work between islands 28.29. Enemy using a new periscope as shown  [sketch] ← glasses. The base of red can be seen through loop hole. The glasses rest on the loop hole. 3 new steel plates have been erected at intervals of about 10x at S28 a.6.8. Probably M.G. loopholes as they are large. Man seen wearing cap similar in shape to our R.F.C. - blue in colour with yellow band. Badge like N.F. or Grenade. An Officer going his rounds showed at 2 places for a moment. A shot was fired & he waved his cane. Wire patrol continued its work. 2 reconnoitring patrols have nothing to report. Officers patrol went out 12-30 a.m. to watch suspected snipers post. Returned 5-30 a.m. 30x wiring done in front of islands 31 + 14. Bomb store constructed island 31. Work on Parados continued. Number boards put up in island 30A. 30B. Gooseberries put in gaps in wire in front of O.B.L. Boards put in parapet to show where gaps are. E.C.	

Instructions regarding War Diaries and Intelligence Summaries are contained in F. S. Regs., Part II. and the Staff Manual respectively. Title Pages will be prepared in manuscript.

WAR DIARY
or
INTELLIGENCE SUMMARY
(Erase heading not required.)

Army Form C. 2118

Place	Date	Hour	Summary of Events and Information	Remarks and references to Appendices
Trenches Festubert Left Sub-sector	10.6.16		About 12 Whizz Bangs fell behind islands 36-38 & more behind cover trench about mid day. Some of retaliation for artillery operation 12-45 a.m. was directed at Cover Trench. No damage done. Snipers broke enemy periscope. Snipers have caused enemy trouble, apparently. Yesterday his snipers concentrated on our snipers plates in left cover trench with help of telescopic periscope. Artillery damaged enemy parapet considerably at S 28 a 3.2. Two snipers crept into ditch between right & left cover trenches during the morning, claim to have dislodged enemy snipers from 2 loopholes in old building at S 28 a 3.6½. 2 snipers were seen there. At 8-30 pm a burst like that of a T.M. heard in enemy wire at S 22 c 6.5. Officers reconnoitring patrol out from island 24 at 9.30 pm. Enemy patrol suspected. Patrol returned & reported another patrol went out. No enemy patrol was seen. The patrol reconnoitred enemy wire which is strong, front wire being 2'6" thick, made of gooseberries fixed on stakes 3' high. Wiring continued outside island 32. Also between islands 20-22. Firesteps erected in breastworks joining islands 34-36. Work on parados continued. Duck boards raised & drains cleared in O.B.L.	
Do.	11/6/16		Quiet day. Battn relieved by 17th KRR's. Relief complete 11-30 pm. Battn marched to billets at R.13. Bethune Combined Sheet. All passed off without incident.	
Billets at R.13. Bethune Combined Sheet	12/6/16		Day spent quietly in billets. Some rain. Roads bad	
	13/6/16		A memorial service under divisional arrangements in memory of LORD KITCHENER was cancelled owing to bad weather. Day spent in billets. Working parties under R.E. Battn at Vieille Chapelle	
Do.	14/6/16		Orders received to be in readiness to move on or about 15/6/16.	
Do.	15/6/16		Battn at Vieille Chapelle. Orders received to move tomorrow to E.4 area (Bethune) Cancelled, & ordered to go on night of 16/17 to Hingette. W.16.17. Bethune Combined Sheet.	
Do and HINGETTE W.16.17.	16/6/16		Battn marched off at 8-30 a.m. Marched by Brigade from X.1.d.7.8. to HINGETTE. Orders received to march to billets at CANTRAINNE on 17th and to billets E.4. on 18th. It was discovered that billets in E.4 would be vacant by 3 p.m. on 17th. Permission received to go straight there and not billet at CANTRAINNE.	
Do and E.4.	17/6/16		Battn marched off at 10.30 a.m. Bivouacked for 3 hours and had dinners at Mondoke Farm W.21.d.7.1. Marched into billets at E4 at 3 p.m. Some difficulty in the billeting and not settled in till about 8 pm. Weather good. Roads good.	

Instructions regarding War Diaries and Intelligence Summaries are contained in F. S. Regs., Part II. and the Staff Manual respectively. Title Pages will be prepared in manuscript.

WAR DIARY
or
INTELLIGENCE SUMMARY
(Erase heading not required.)

Army Form C. 2118

Place	Date	Hour	Summary of Events and Information	Remarks and references to Appendices
E.4. Bethune Combined Sheet	18-6-16.		Day spent in billets. A general overhauling of kit and stores of the Batt'n. Weather holding good. Roads good	J.L.
DO.	19-6-16		Day in billets. Weather good. Training such as to make men physically fit and hard. Route marches, physical training, etc	J.L.
			Day spent in route marching and training in billets. Weather good. 2nd Lt J THURGOOD reported for duty	J.L.
DO	20-6-16.		Working parties on new Shooting range. Route marches and training in billets	J.L.
DO	21-6-16.		Working parties on range. Bombing training - Inspection by DADOS 35th Division	J.L.
DO.	22-6-16		Day fine.	J.L.
			Bombing practice. Work on Range. Route marching training in billets.	J.L.
DO	23-6-16.		Baths at GONNEHEM. V17a 9.2. Bethune Comb'd Sheet. Bombing. Shooting. Training	J.L.
DO	24-6-16.		in billets. Route Marching.	
DO	25-6-16.		Parade Services. No training. M.O.'s report for previous week on Sanitary work done - 117 fly proof latrines have been fixed. Several others are almost ready & will be fixed as soon as possible. Grease traps have been made in several places where needed. No incinerators needed, but existing ones improved. Stagnant pools of water sprayed with cresol. Feces from billets burnt. In some cases buried. 4 Cases Evacuated to Field Ambulance. 6 Officers medically examined for Flying Corps.	J.L.
DO.	26-6-16		Baths at V17d 9.2. 2nd Lt J. MARSHALL. 2nd Lt H.E. KEETON. 2nd Lt S.A.C. THORNE reported for duty. - Shooting. Bombing. Training in billets.	J.L.
DO.	27-6-16		Brigade horse show. Batt'n carried off 5 first prizes in 8 events. Weather bad and not all the programme could be carried out. - Shooting & bombing in morning. 2nd Lt de WITT received orders to go to England to join Reserve Batt'n. 2nd Lt BEST appointed Bombing Officer in this place.	J.L.

1875 Wt. W593/826 1,000,000 4/15 J.B.C. & A. A.D.S.S./Forms/C. 2118.

Army Form C. 2118

Instructions regarding War Diaries and Intelligence Summaries are contained in F. S. Regs., Part II. and the Staff Manual respectively. Title Pages will be prepared in manuscript.

WAR DIARY
or
INTELLIGENCE SUMMARY
(Erase heading not required.)

Place	Date	Hour	Summary of Events and Information	Remarks and references to Appendices
BETHUNE	28-6-16.		A Field day which had been arranged was cancelled. Orders to be prepared to move at any time were received. 605 Pte Devitt and 306 Pte Cox were complimented in Brigade Orders for act of courage in stopping a runaway horse. 6 Officers before a Medical Board in view of transfer to R.F.C. Transport left at 6 pm. under Capt. BANKS.	EP
DO.	29-6-16		Training in Billets under Coy arrangements. Weather good.	EP
DO.	30-6-16		Training in Billets under Coy arrangements. Weather good.	EP

1875 Wt. W593/826 1,000,000 4/15 J.B.C. & A. A.D.S.S./Forms/C. 2118.

CONFIDENTIAL,

W A R D I A R Y

of

17TH (S) BN. WEST YORKSHIRE REGT,

From. 1st May 1916 to 31st May 1916

......

VOLUME IV.

Army Form C. 2118.

Instructions regarding War Diaries and Intelligence Summaries are contained in F. S. Regs., Part II. and the Staff Manual respectively. Title Pages will be prepared in manuscript.

WAR DIARY
or
INTELLIGENCE SUMMARY

(Erase heading not required.)

Place	Date	Hour	Summary of Events and Information	Remarks and references to Appendices
Les LOBES.	1/5/16.		Working parties at PACAUT & RICHEBOURG, latter for 2 days, and men billeted away from Battn. – Day spent in billets. Weather hot Roads good. E.P.	
			Working parties at Pacaut and Richebourg, latter for 2 days, men billeted away. – Training in billets. E.P.	
DO.	2/5/16		Working party at Pacaut. C.O Lewis Gun Officer and Bombing Officer, visited new line. Training in billets. E.P.	
DO	3/5/16		106th Bde Concentration March. Route from Q.9.b.5.0 via cross roads N of CALONNE Church, Q.5.b.5.5,	
DO	4/5/16.		Q.11.b.6.2. Q.12.c.0.0. – Brigadier General O'Donnell congratulated the Brigade on its smart appearance. Weather & roads good. E.P.	
DO.	5/5/16		Working party at Pacaut. Meeting of Officers at 4.30 p.m. 1 Officer per Coy and 1 N.C.O per Platoon went into the line to take over. Weather and roads good. E.P.	
DO and TRENCHES.	6/5/16		Battn took over left Subsector, Ferme du Bois Section from 16th Cheshire Regt. X Coy Rt Coy – Part of S.16.3 and all S.16.4. Y Coy centre – S.16.5. S.10.1. Z Coy Left – S.10.2. S.10.3. W Coy in Reserve in Posts. Relief complete 10-15 p.m. Lewis Gunners, Snipers, Signallers & Bombers relieved before noon. Day fine & roads good – Night quiet on arrival in the line. E.P.	
~~TRENCHES~~	~~7/5/16.~~		Lewis Gunners kept up fire on gaps in enemy wire and parapet made by artillery, at S.10.c.9.2. & S.10.c.0.5. A fast enemy MG located at S.16.a.6.4. Another MG fired on about S.10.c.0.3. and was not seen or heard again. Enemy wire in most places appears not good. – Work on Firing step, Snipers put in loop hole to command gap in wire. Old battle emplacement renovated to night emplacement begun at S.10.c.9.7. E.C.	
TRENCHES	7/5/16		Scheme of MGs as handed over found to be unsatisfactory for covering gaps, and new scheme was drafted and guns altered accordingly. Lewis Guns traversed enemy wire and parapet during the night. Vickers guns fired indirect fire from S.8.a.3.3. to target S.16.d.3.8. Enemy fired about 20 rounds HE between 11.30 a.m. and 12 noon on to Pall Mall, Copse, Right Guards & Factory Keeps. – Officers patrol out from S.16.5 up to enemy wire. The going was good, shell holes & broken ground affording cover. Sounds of driving of stakes and pumping heard in enemy line. Enemy wire reported strengthened at S.10.c.8½.2. – Concertina pattern, about 15 yds long and over parapet. – Working party fired on at S.16.a.6½.2. Much work at this point being done by enemy. Two men seen digging in Ferme du Bois, who disappeared on being fired at. 2 men seen at S.16.d.7.9½, one at 4 p.m. who disappeared on being fired at. – Much wiring done during the night along all our front. Reserve Coy continued work on Dug outs & Fire Steps. – Coys working in conjunction with R.E. E.C.	

Instructions regarding War Diaries and Intelligence Summaries are contained in F. S. Regs., Part II. and the Staff Manual respectively. Title Pages will be prepared in manuscript.

WAR DIARY
or
INTELLIGENCE SUMMARY
(Erase heading not required.)

Army Form C. 2118

Place	Date	Hour	Summary of Events and Information	Remarks and references to Appendices
Trenches.	8/5/16.		Combined operation between our artillery and T.M.s 10-30 p.m. – 10-45 p.m. Several direct hits on enemy parapet by T.M.s. Lewis Guns cooperated, to keep enemy under so that he could not locate T.M.s and see shells coming. Enemy retaliated with H.E. on supports – Bute St. Copse Keep, Rue du Bois & Pall Mall Keep. No damage to front line. One dug out hit in Bute St. Glenn St. C. trench blocked for 5x. At 5 p.m. enemy landed a shell in parapet at S10.1. S10.2 (junction of..) – New disposition of M.G.s appears successful as no fresh work has been done on gaps in enemy wire + parapet. 2 Germans seen examining posts at S.10.d.5.5. They disappeared on being fired at by Sniper. Two Red + White flags have been placed in enemy parapet about 125x apart in Boars Head S.16.a.5.7. S.16.a.5.8½. A new snipers loophole constructed during night above enemy parapet at S.10.c.9½.5. – Enemy seen working on his reserve line + behind front line trench S.16.a.5.6. Snipers fired on latter party and dispersed it. A German looked over an uncovered loop hole plate at S10.c.8.2 at 2-30 p.m. He wore a mask and was using glasses. Sniper fired and he rapidly disappeared. Our Snipers concentrated on enemy loop holes between S10.c.9.3 and S10.d.3.6. where enemy had been troublesome. All sniping from that quarter ceased. Sniper smashed enemy periscope. Much more seen ^moving^ from enemy support line. S10.c.9.3 - S10.d.3.6. New Enemy M.G. appeared at S.10.d.5.6. at 4 p.m. It was at once fired at and nothing heard of it after 9-30 p.m. Flashes of electric torch or flash lamp were seen about S.16.a.2.3. Lewis Gunners at S16.a.2.2. report shells which fell in our wire about 10.45 p.m. affected their eyes and their heads became heavy. Enemy sent up Red Rockets at 10-30 p.m. immediately after our guns had opened fire – evidently a call for retaliation. Work under R.E. – Parapet repaired. Standard dug out finished in Bute St. Work on Fire Steps in Supporting points and Keeps.	E.L.
Do.	9/5/16.		Day and night unusually quiet on both sides. Officers patrol went out from S16.a.2½. to try and locate enemy M.G. suspected at S16.a.6½.1. Gun did not fire. A large working party seen on enemy parapet. Lewis Guns opened on them, hoping also to draw fire of M.G., but they failed to do so. 2 patrol M.G.s in enemy line between S.16.a.6.1 and S.16.a.5½.6. Sentry at junction of S10.2. S10.3. reported enemy patrol about 20x from our parapet at 2 a.m. Lewis Guns swept the ground, but nothing could be seen at daylight. Enemy exposed dummies during the day – one with steel helmet on, shaped like a sou-wester, + coloured like our own. Sniper located at S.10.d.0.6. – Work on parapets, parados, traverses – Building, filling of sandbags continued under R.E. 2 new dug outs begun in S10.1. + S16.5. Wiring parties out at night. Damage done by bombardment previous night was made good. Work on dug outs + fire steps continued	G.C.

1875 Wt. W593/826 1,000,000 4/15 J.B.C. & A. A.D.S.S./Forms/C. 2118.

Instructions regarding War Diaries and Intelligence Summaries are contained in F. S. Regs., Part II. and the Staff Manual respectively. Title Pages will be prepared in manuscript.

WAR DIARY
or
INTELLIGENCE SUMMARY
(Erase heading not required.)

Army Form C. 2118

Place	Date	Hour	Summary of Events and Information	Remarks and references to Appendices
Trenches and Billets at RICHEBOURG.	10/5/16		CAPT. A.B. CRAWFORD, O.C. W Coy, killed by Shrapnel in ~~Cope~~ Butt St about 12-45 pm. – Some shelling during the day. Relieved by 19th D.L.I. at night. Relief complete 10.15 pm. Batt^n went into billets at Richebourg. W Coy took over Posts – Dogs. S 9 b. 2½. 8½. Edwards S 9. a 9. 8. Hens, S. 3. d. 1. 3. Richebourg S 2. c 3. 1. Hunter. S. 8. a. 2. 3. Scott S. 8. a. 2. 0. – Grotto + Angle S. 2. a. 8. 8	
Richebourg.	11/5/16.		Day spent in billets. 2 working parties of 2 Platoons each at 8 p.m. Baths at Richebourg. S. 8. a. 7. 9. Apcumptd buried at St Vaast.	EC
DO.	12/5/16		working parties – 2 Platoons during the day – 4 during the night. Lt. HEPPER. and 4 men went to Corps Sniping Course at Steenbecque. Baths.	EC
DO.	13/5/16		working parties as on 12th arranged, but 2 at night put off owing to an operation and expected retaliation. Retaliation came 10-10 pm, over billets. Nobody was hurt and no damage was done. – Baths.	EC. EC
Do and Trenches.	14/5/16		Batt^n relieve D.L.I in Left Subsector, Ferme du Bois Section. Relief complete by 10-5 pm. Enemy MG silenced at S.10 d. 1½. 5½. about 9 p.m. Enemy periscope smashed by our sniper. Enemy active with MG's till 11 pm. Officers patrol out S. 16. 3 to examine enemy's wire. Sounds of hammering heard in enemy trenches. Enemy patrol of about 14 men seen by a patrol of which went out at S. 10. 1. Our patrol of 1 NCO and 5 men returned and reported but on lights being sent up nothing could be seen. Work in progress about S.10. d. 1. 5. was heard. Wiring parties out. Mining suspected at S. 10. c. 8. 5. + Boars head. Listeners heard sounds as of sawing at S. 10 c. 8. 5. At S. 16. a. 7. 2½. what appears to be an advanced trench in course of construction – about 50^x long – was seen. 2 men seen at S. 10 c 9. 3. 3 dummy loop holes discovered in enemy line at S. 10. d. 1. 5. – Work on parados, traverses fire steps etc.	EC
Trenches	15/5/16.		Lewis Guns at S. 10. c 8½. 6. and S 10. d. 0. 7½. opened fire on wiring party at S 10. d. 1. 5. at 1-50 p.m. Enemy MG located at S. 16. a. 5. 7. Lewis Gun moved from S. 16 a. 5½. 6½ to S 16. a. 2. 4. to cope with it. 2 Enemy periscopes broken. Enemy MG's active at night. Officers patrol left S. 10. 2 at 1 a.m. Returned to report enemy wiring party which was fired on by Lewis Guns. Again tin which had been used as a Very light fell in our lines at S 10. 2. Suspected MG emplacement at S 10. d. 1. 5½. A wooden structure seen at S. 16. a. 5½. 5½. Patrol reported enemy wiring at this spot. Enemy new wire seen at S. 10. d. 1½. 5. Enemy exposed dummy periscopes. At 10 a.m. enemy seen carrying planks and sandbags behind the line. Earth thrown over parapet at S. 16 a. 6½. 2 at 3.30 pm.	

1875 Wt. W593/826 1,000,000 4/15 J.B.C. & A. A.D.S.S./Forms/C. 2118.

WAR DIARY
or
INTELLIGENCE SUMMARY
(Erase heading not required.)

Army Form C. 2118

Instructions regarding War Diaries and Intelligence Summaries are contained in F. S. Regs., Part II. and the Staff Manual respectively. Title Pages will be prepared in manuscript.

Place	Date	Hour	Summary of Events and Information	Remarks and references to Appendices
Trenches.	15/5/16 cont^d		At S.16.a.5.8½ a wooden hammer (Maul) was being swung up and down at 5 p.m. Five shots were fired and the work ceased. 2 Pigeons seen at 11-25 a.m. at S.10.c.9½.4½ flying South. Wiring parties out at night. Snipers let in new loop hole at S.16.3 commanding Boars Head. 2 Standard dugouts prepared for in Bute St. + brick barriers added to Officers Dugout. Work on screen in Rue du Bois was continued. Posts + railings erected to Bridge over ditch to Medical aid Post. Sand bags filled ready to block Copse St if necessary. Work under R.E. during the day. E.P.	
Do.	16/5/16		Snipers claim one victim – a man wearing blue round cap with small badge. Enemy sniper fired at our Periscope at 7-40 pm. A miss was signalled. He fired again + was located. Officers patrol went out from S.16.a.1½.5. with object of meeting suspected enemy patrol at 1-30 a.m. No patrol met. Night was light – moon bright – Our aeroplanes practised night flying. Enemy shelled Factory Keep S.9.d.5.2. and Rue du Bois about mid day. 6 HE fell about Guards Keep, S.10.c.4.8. but did much damage to parapet. At 5-15 Railhead behind Bute St, S.10.a.6.4 was shelled with 77 mm? One shell fell in and others near Factory Keep, S.9.d.5.2 at 5-20 p.m. At 5-45 p.m 2 Salvoes of Shrapnel burst on junction of Copse St and Rue du Bois S.10.a.4.0. Enemy MG emplacements definitely located at S.16.a.6½.3 S.16.a.5¼.6¾. S.10.d.1.6. Wiring parties of enemy were heard by our listening posts. No sounds of mining detected in Boars Head. A bridged gap seen at S.16.a.5¼.5¼. – 3 feet wide. Enemy wire thick at this point. Another Sally port discovered at S.16.a.3¼.7¼. Enemy exposed dummy figures. Enemy wire broken down at S.16.a.5½.5. Coils of wire were thrown over parapet at this spot about 8 p.m. – 4 Germans seen in "no mans land" at S.16.a.4.4. They scrambled back to their line when fired on. – Wiring was done in front of our right and centre Coys. S.10.1. S.16.5. S.16.4. S.16.3. Much work on parapets + parados. Double snipers loophole for observer + sniper let in in Boars Head about S.16.a.4.7. E.P.	
Do.	17/5/16		Intermittent artillery activity throughout the day. Aeroplanes night flying. Snipers claim one victim. Man seen working on parapet at S.10.c.9½.5 was heard to cry out when fired on by L.G. Rue du Bois + Copse St shelled with Shrapnel + Whizz bangs, + Edward Road with HE from 8.15 a.m – 9.15 a.m. Enemy's wire patrolled + found to be thick + good. Sap discovered running under knife rests to a listening post, behind a fallen tree. Empty cartridge cases found there. Attempt to test Battery covering S.16.4. was unsuccessful, owing to broken telephone connection. Small working party at S.10.c.6.5 dispersed by Snipers. Officer + N.C.O patrolled in morning went up to 30x of enemy line. – Double snipers loophole let in at S.16.4. Wiring along whole Batt. front S.10.3 – S.16.3. Work on Medical aid Post in Bute St + on Coy dugout. E.P.	

Instructions regarding War Diaries and Intelligence Summaries are contained in F. S. Regs., Part II. and the Staff Manual respectively. Title Pages will be prepared in manuscript.

WAR DIARY
or
INTELLIGENCE SUMMARY

(Erase heading not required.)

Army Form C. 2118

Place	Date	Hour	Summary of Events and Information	Remarks and references to Appendices
Trenches + Billets Richebourg St Vaast	18/5/16		Batt^n relieved by 19th D.L.I. Snipers relieved by 9 a.m. Signallers by 10.30 a.m. Lewis Gunners + Bombers by 12 noon. Same billets & Posts taken over at Richebourg as formerly. Relief complete by 10.30 pm. Capt Rason, OC Z Coy, wounded about 12.30 pm. E.C.	
	19/5/16		Day spent quietly in billets. Weather good. Baths at Richebourg St Vaast E.C. Capt Wilcher took over command Z Coy. Baths. Working Parties	
Richebourg St Vaast.	20/5/16		Baths. Working Parties. Church Services for X + Y Coys. Lt Rachie [?] posted to W Coy. 2nd Lt Stead to Y Coy	
Do	21/5/16		2nd Lt Wilkinson to Z Coy. Day spent in billets. Weather good.	
Do and La Grove Rumeuse [?] R13.	22/5/16		Batt^n relieved in Bde reserve billets by 18th Lancashire Fusiliers. Batt^n marched by Coys independently to billets at R.13. (Bethune Combined Sheet) 1 working party provided for R.E. Archbishop of Canterbury inspected the Batt^n at 6 pm. E.C.	
Billets at R13.	23/5/16		Parades under Coy arrangements. Day spent at work in billets. E.C.	
Do	24/5/16		Working parties. – 2nd Lt de Lussa [?] posted W Coy, 2nd Lt Rendell, 2nd Lt Russell X Coy, 2nd Lt Mitchell Y Coy, 2nd Lt Dickinson Z Coy. E.C.	
Do	25/5/16		Working Party. Training under Coy arrangements. Wiring by all Coys. E.C.	
Do	26/5/16		Working Parties. 2nd Lt Stead took over command Y Coy during absence on leave of Capt Huffam. E.C. Training under Coy arrangements.	
Do	27/5/16		Working parties. Training under Coy arrangements. E.C.	
Do + Trenches	28/5/16		Working parties. Services for all denominations. All arrangements cancelled, and Batt^n received orders to relieve left subsector Festubert Section, the same night. This was completed by 12-20 am. Night passed quietly. E.C.	
Trenches S.22.1 S.28.1 S.27.2 S.27.1 Trench Map Area G.	29/5/16		W and Y Coys in Old British line in reserve, from S.21.a.[illegible].2½ – S.26.d.3.9¾. Z Coy left S.22.1 and half X Coy on the Right in the line, S.27.a.1.8½ – S.28.a.1.5½. (Trench Map Area G) Artillery + aeroplane activity on both sides. Enemy fired 6 T.M.s on our left about 11 pm. 6 men were wounded. We retaliated with artillery and Rifle Grenades, 13 of which landed in enemy trench. – X Coy holding islands 14–28, Z Coy 29–38. Each has platoon in Richmond Terrace. Much wiring done. Heightening of fire step. Work on Parados + duck boards. Lines cleaned up. SAA + Bomb stores built in O.B.L. E.C.	

1875 Wt. W593/826 1,000,000 4/15 J.B.C. & A. A.D.S.S./Forms/C. 2118.

Instructions regarding War Diaries and Intelligence Summaries are contained in F. S. Regs., Part II. and the Staff Manual respectively. Title Pages will be prepared in manuscript.

WAR DIARY
or
INTELLIGENCE SUMMARY
(Erase heading not required.)

Army Form C. 2118

Place	Date	Hour	Summary of Events and Information	Remarks and references to Appendices
Trenches Festubert Section. Left Subsection.	30/5/16.		2 Snipers located at S.22.c.6.1. One had on light blue cap with silver and blue badge, other a green Prussian peakless cap with round silver badge. Both wore goggles. Snipers fired 2 shots. They dispersed from behind their loophole, two further firing came from them. Enemy periscope smashed by sniper. Enemy T.M.'s again fired on S.22.1 about 8 p.m. Retaliation by Stokes gun and artillery silenced them. Officers Patrol went out from island 24, 11.15 – 1.15. Enemy's trip wire was cut in places about S.28.a.0.0. Sounds of driving of stakes and much work going on in enemy front line. Trial wiring done 70 yards by left line Coy between support of islands 29-30A. Also wiring in front of S.27.b.8.3½ – S.27.b.9.4½. Continuous aprons put up, and ditches and old German communication trench blocked by "gooseberries". Trenches partially reclaimed between islands 32.33 – S.28.a.3.8 – S.28.a.3.9½. Work on parados in O.B. Line. Snipers loop hole let in at S.26.b.4.2. Violent artillery duel on our left on Neuve Chapelle and Richebourg between 7.30 and 10-15 p.m.	
Do.	31/5/16		Lewis Gunners, Signallers & Snipers in island line relieved during night by 19th D.L.I. Relief complete by 2 a.m. Enemy shelled Shetland Rd Communication trench lightly during the day. Ruined house at S.28.a.3.6½ reported held by snipers and mound near it at S.28.a.3½ 7 reported used at night. Very lights are always sent up from the sap running from island 32 to enemy line and a M.G. was knocked out there by one of our Lewis Guns on night of 30/31. Patrol of 1 officer + 4 men out at 9.30 from island 30. S.28.a.3.5½ to reconnoitre. The old communication trench found to be unoccupied. Snipers Post on N. side of this trench is a shell hole. Tracks in the grass were found running from shell hole to German line on one side & to the C.T. trench on the other. Other Snipers Post is a large pile of bricks. 2 loopholes found & signs of recent occupation. 2 more patrols out. One inspected mound at S.28.a.5.8 which was not occupied. A wiring party out in front of S.27.b.8.3½ – S.27.b.9.4½ was approached by small enemy patrol who retired on seeing them. Enemy M.G.s then opened fire. Wiring to amount of 250x has now been done in front of islands. It is still weak in places. Work on parados, duckboards, wiring etc in O.B. line. Parapet strengthened in O.B. line and at S.21.d.1.9 Rt line Coy. Connecting trenches between parts of cover trench were partially reclaimed. ~~Batt" relieved by 19th D.L.I.~~ [illegible signature]	

1875 Wt. W593/826 1,000,000 4/15 J.B.C. & A. A.D.S.S./Forms/C. 2118.

106th Bde.

35th Div.

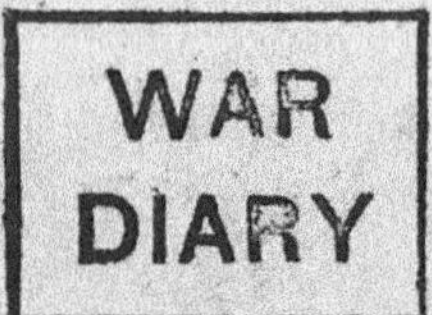

17th BATTALION

WEST YORKS REGIMENT

1st to 31st JULY 1916.

Report on Operations 29/30th July in G.S.Diary

Confidential.

W A R D I A R Y

-- of --

17TH (S) BATTN. WEST YORKSHIRE REGT.,

From 1st July 1916 to 31st July 1916.

VOLUME 6

Instructions regarding War Diaries and Intelligence Summaries are contained in F. S. Regs., Part II. and the Staff Manual respectively. Title Pages will be prepared in manuscript.

WAR DIARY
or
~~INTELLIGENCE SUMMARY~~
(Erase heading not required.)

Army Form C. 2118

Place	Date	Hour	Summary of Events and Information	Remarks and references to Appendices
BETHUNE	1-7-16		M.O's Report for week ending 1-7-16. "Besides ordinary work 15 Fly proof Cabinets have been fixed. Others still needed but tools having gone forward on transport, it is difficult to continue the work. Fly traps and butter muslin have been indented for for Officers Messes. A case of infectious disease – German measles – occurred amongst the Officers [LT HOGGETT]. The billet has been disinfected by sanitary squad, 37th DIV and the bed clothes boiled. Notice of the infection has been posted on the door of the house. 6 cases evacuated to Field ambulance during the week (sd) A.A. Watson M.O. i/c 17th West Yorks Regt.	
			Day spent in training in billets. Weather good.	E.C.
DO.	2-7-16		Church parades in the morning. Orders to move received 9-10 pm. Battn entrained at CHOCQUES at 11-30 pm. Train No 2. Weather & roads good.	E.C.
LE SOUICH.	3-7-16		Battn detrained at FRÉVENT [about 8 miles S of ST POL] at 3-30 a.m. Breakfast outside the station. Marched away to billets at LE SOUICH [5 miles N of DOULLENS] at 7 a.m. Weather & roads good. Arrived in billets about 10-30 a.m. Packs brought on to Bde HQrs at IVERGNY under Brigade arrangements	E.C.
Do.	4-7-16		Day spent quietly in billets. Orders received that Battn will move tomorrow	E.C.
Do	5-7-16		Battn paraded at 8-15 p.m. From road junction S. of L in LUCHEUX the Battn marched in Brigade via L'Esperance, – HALLOY – Road fork ¾ mile N.E of FAMECHON Church, AUTHIE to camp in BOIS DU WARNIMONT about 7½ miles S.E.E of DOULLENS.	E.C.
BOIS du WARNIMONT.	6-7-16		Battn arrived in camp about 2-30 a.m. and settled into hutments and tents. Day spent in sleeping, cleaning up and preparations for training.	E.C.
DO.	7-7-16		Day spent in training under Coy arrangements. Much rain and camp very muddy	E.C.
DO.	8-7-16		Day spent in training until noon. Men allowed the afternoon free. Rain at intervals.	E.C.
DO.	9-7-16		Church parades for all denominations. Day fine weather very good & camp dried up quickly. – Orders received to move by Bde in morning to Puchevillers. Orders cancelled. Orders received to march as a Battn to Beaussart to work – & come back to billets in Bertrancourt. The Brigade to be split up for work under 4th Division	E.C.

1875 Wt. W593/826 1,000,000 4/15 J.B.C. & A. A.D.S.S./Forms/C. 2118.

Army Form C. 2118

Instructions regarding War Diaries and Intelligence Summaries are contained in F. S. Regs., Part II. and the Staff Manual respectively. Title Pages will be prepared in manuscript.

WAR DIARY or INTELLIGENCE SUMMARY

(Erase heading not required.)

Place	Date	Hour	Summary of Events and Information	Remarks and references to Appendices
			Medical Officers report for week ending 9-7-16:– Sanitary arrangements improved and more latrines made at LE SOUICH. While billeted in BOIS DU WARNIMONT a new incinerator was built and a large quantity of rubbish burned and buried. 2 large refuse pits filled in. 6 cases evacuated to F.A. during the week: (Sd) C.A. Walton M.O. 1/c 17 West Yorks Regt	
Bois du Warnimont and Varennes. P25 d. 3.7 Sheet 57.d	10-7-16		Battn marched from Bois du Warnimont at 8-15 a.m. towards BEAUSSART. Billets arranged at BRETINCOURT when the order came that the Brigade would march to VARENNES. The Battn stopped in a field outside BRETINCOURT and had dinners. Orders came to move off at 3-15 p.m. Battn arrived VARENNES at about 5 p.m. and marched into camp (of shelters) Packs arrived on lorries soon afterwards.	E.C.
VARENNES.	11-7-16		Training in Camp. Weather good.	E.C.
Do	12-7-16		Battn marched away to billets at BRESLE at 8-30 p.m. in Brigade. March uneventful. Major P.S. HALL left to take over command of 13th Cheshire Regt.	E.C.
BRESLE + Bois des CELESTINES	13-7-16		Battn marched off at 10 a.m. to BOIS DES CELESTINES. to hutments. Orders received to move again at 6 p.m. Marched to BILLON COPSE F30. Sheet 62 D. and bivouaced for night.	E.C.
+ BILLON COPSE TALUS BOISE	14-7-16		Battn marched at 11 a.m. to TALUS BOISE and bivouaced on E side about A15.a. Montauban sheet. Working parties, 2 reliefs of 60 men – loaded T.M. bombs at CARNOY in afternoon and evening.	E.C.
Do.	15-7-16		Battn in reserve at TALUS BOISE. Working party 200 men to BERNAFAY WOOD S.28.29. during night with object of laying cable. Owing to heavy shelling little work was done	E.C.
Do	16-7-16		Orders received to be prepared to make an attack on GINCHY in conjunction with remainder of 106th Bde. Orders cancelled. Working parties. 2 reliefs 60 men. to 106 Bde Forward Dump.	E.C.
Do.	17-7-16.		Working party 60 men to BERNAFAY WOOD at night to lay cable. LT. W H. COLDECK wounded. 4 men killed and others wounded. Little work done owing to heavy shelling. Battn stood to arms 10-30 p.m. – 12.30 a.m. Weather continues good.	E.C.
Do and SOUTH TRENCH. S27. d	18-7-16		Battn marched at about 6 p.m. under orders of 26th Bde to SOUTH TRENCH, – old German support line S of MONTAUBAN S.27.d. Severe shelling throughout the night. Battn in expectation of being moved up.	E.C.

1875 Wt. W593/826 1,000,000 4/15 J.B.C. & A. A.D.S.S./Forms/C. 2118.

Instructions regarding War Diaries and Intelligence Summaries are contained in F. S. Regs., Part II. and the Staff Manual respectively. Title Pages will be prepared in manuscript.

WAR DIARY

~~or~~

~~INTELLIGENCE SUMMARY~~

(Erase heading not required.)

Army Form C. 2118

Place	Date	Hour	Summary of Events and Information	Remarks and references to Appendices
SOUTH TRENCH S.27.d	19-7-16		Y and Z Coys attached from 4 pm to the 9th Seaforth Highlanders (Pioneers) by orders of 8th Bde for consolidation work and digging of trenches N. of MONTAUBAN. CAPT B.L. WILCHER, O.C. Z Coy, wounded by shrapnel. 3 Platoons W Coy under orders of 27th Bde, carried lights, flares and wire to South Street – in Delville Wood. Y + Z Coys relieved in Montauban by 2nd Royal Scots marched back to Camp at CAFTET WOOD S.W. of Carnoy. F.18.c. Sheet 62.d.	
DO.	20-7-16		Battn did Salvage work throughout the day and buried men of various regiments which had been left lying in the vicinity of South trench. Y + Z Coys recalled from camp. The Battn by this time under orders of 53rd Bde.	
CAFTET WOOD	21-7-16		Battn relieved about 3 a.m. by a Battn of Shropshire L.I. and marched back to CAFTET WOOD arriving about 6 a.m. CAPT. S HUFFAM took over command 19th D.L.I.	
Do and trench A1.c.d	22-7-16		Battn moved about 8 pm. to the old S.W. Montauban trench A1.c.d. W Coy moved forward and took up position in Montauban Alley. S27.c.a.b. Battn now under orders of 9th Bde	
DO.	23-7-16		X Coy moved up to South trench S.27.a about 10 a.m. Owing to severe shelling the Coy vacated the trench about mid day and joined W Coy in Montauban Alley. W Coy went forward as a working party to DELVILLE WOOD with the object of digging an advanced trench. No guides were met and no covering party had been put out. The Coy was therefore employed in carrying ammunition to the front line trench in Delville Wood. X Coy provided carrying party 40 men for wire to Delville Wood. Remainder X Coy returned to trench A1.c.d about 1.30 a.m. (24th)	
Do and Bernafay Wood	24-7-16		Orders received for the Battn to move off and take up position N.E. of Bernafay Wood. Battn minus W Coy + 40 men X Coy + 25 X Coy (at 106 Bde forward dump) moved off at 2.30 a.m. and took up position in C. trench NE of Bernafay Wood S29 a. S23 c. at 4 a.m. Severe shelling throughout the day + casualties comparatively heavy. Message received 9 pm. German attack expected & the Battn to hold itself ready to move up in support. Outposts posted along ridge S23 a S23 c throughout the night.	

1875 Wt. W593/826 1,000,000 4/15 J.B.C. & A. A.D.S.S./Forms/C. 2118.

Instructions regarding War Diaries and Intelligence Summaries are contained in F. S. Regs., Part II. and the Staff Manual respectively. Title Pages will be prepared in manuscript.

WAR DIARY
or
INTELLIGENCE SUMMARY
(Erase heading not required.)

Army Form C. 2118

Place	Date	Hour	Summary of Events and Information	Remarks and references to Appendices
Bernafay Wood	25-7-16		Orders received 2 a.m. that Battn could stand down and that when 9th Bde should be relieved by 99th the Battn would come under orders of 106th Bde. Battn employed during day on Salvage work and burying of dead. 8 pm. Orders received from 106th Bde to march back to Camp at CAFTET WOOD. Battn marched through barrage of gas + tear shells, and gas helmets had to be worn. Arrived in camp 11 pm. EL.	
			[M.O. report week ending 22-7-16. "No special sanitary work was done. Trench latrines used. Shell holes utilised for getting rid of rubbish and afterwards filled in. Among cases evacuated were 8 shell shock and several with quite slight injuries." Lt Watson M.O. i/c 17th W Yorks R.	
CAFTET WOOD + Casement trench	26-7-16		G.O.C. 35th Div. addressed Officers 106 Bde at Bde HQrs 11.30 a.m. Battn moved at 7 pm. to Casement trench. A 10 a & b. EL.	
Casement trench + Caftet Wood	27-7-16		Working party 200 men reported at 2 pm. to N.W. corner Bernafay Wood for trench digging. 50 reported at 2 pm. to S.28.d.4.1 as further trench digging party. 50 men reported same place at 6 pm. for same purpose. Battn moved back to camp Caftet Wood during afternoon under orders 106th Bde. Order received 8 pm. to be ready to move at ½ hours notice to support 2nd Division. Destination Bernafay Wood. EL.	
Caftet Wood	28-7-16		Battn at rest in Caftet Wood. O.C. Coys reconnoitred at 3-15 am up as far as front line trenches Maltz Horn Farm. EL.	
Do and Dublin trench.	29-7-16		Battn moved at 7.30 pm. to Dublin trench A.4.c.d. Continuous preparations throughout night for attack on morrow, for which Battn was in reserve to 89th Bde, Rt Bde of British line attacking S. of Guillemont. The Battn heavily shelled throughout the night with Gas + tear shells. Many men affected. 5 Casualties from shelling. EL.	

Instructions regarding War Diaries and Intelligence Summaries are contained in F. S. Regs., Part II. and the Staff Manual respectively. Title Pages will be prepared in manuscript.

WAR DIARY
or
~~INTELLIGENCE SUMMARY~~
(Erase heading not required.)

Army Form C. 2118

Place	Date	Hour	Summary of Events and Information	Remarks and references to Appendices
Dublin trench and MALTZ HORN Farm trench	30-7-16		At 4-45 a.m. Batt.n left Dublin trench, arriving at Bernafay trench at 5-15 a.m. The trench found to be occupied by Bedfords. The Batt.n lay down in the open. At 6-15 am some of the Bedfords advanced leaving behind 1 Coy. – Batt.n occupied remainder of trench. The other assembly trenches in front found to be still occupied, and Batt.n advanced to hold Maltz Horn Farm trench which was unoccupied. At 6-40 a.m. the Batt.n advanced across the open ~~leaving behind 1 Coy~~ & 3 Coys arriving in Maltz Horn Farm trench between 7-5 a.m. and 7-30 a.m. 1 Coy kept in reserve in Hairpin trench. On arrival O.C. 17th Kings said it was too late to go forward & make an isolated attack, so it was decided to stay in Maltz Horn Farm trench & hold it. At 8 a.m. an Officers patrol went forward to see if it was possible to advance & consolidate the sunken Road. The CO of either Manchesters or Scots Fusiliers considered it impossible, on being consulted by patrol, because of MG fire & sniping, but thought it could be done at night. Batt.n occupied in improving front line trench. About 3 p.m. a telephone message from 89th Bde advised counter attack expected from direction of Arrow Head Copse with object of getting a footing in Trones Wood. 4th Coy moved up into the front line to support other 3, on receipt of this message. Information read that Batt.n would be relieved at 11 p.m. At midnight one Coy (X Coy) sent under orders of 89th Bde to report to HQ Batt.n at junction of Trones Wood – Guillemont Rd with Trones Wood – S.30.a.5.4.	x Corte [illegible]
Maltz Horn Farm trench, Caftet Wood + Sand Pit Valley	31-7-16		Batt.n relieved 4-30 a.m. & marched back to Caftet Wood. Batt.n present by 9 a.m. Orders received to march to SANDPIT VALLEY E18.d F19.a Sheet 62.d. N.E. Batt.n marched at 6 p.m. Camp severely shelled as Batt.n left. 8 casualties. Arrived Sand Pit Valley 8-30 p.m.	
			Casualties since 13th – 10 Officers 306 O.R.	
			No report to 29-7-16. 7 Fly proof latrines erected Caftet Wood Camp. Otherwise little sanitary work done. All water [illegible]	

1875 Wt. W593/826 1,000,000 4/15 J.B.C. & A. A.D.S.S./Forms/C. 2118.

106th Brigade

35th Division.

1/17th BATTALION

WEST YORKS REGIMENT

AUGUST 1 9 1 6

Instructions regarding War Diaries and Intelligence Summaries are contained in F. S. Regs., Part II. and the Staff Manual respectively. Title Pages will be prepared in manuscript.

WAR DIARY
or
INTELLIGENCE SUMMARY
(Erase heading not required.)

Army Form C. 2118.

35
17. W Yorks
Vol 7

Place	Date	Hour	Summary of Events and Information	Remarks and references to Appendices
SAND PIT VALLEY. E.R.d Fg a. Sht 62 D NE.	1-8-16.		Bathing during the morning in the ANCRE. Battn marched at 5-50 pm. via SAND PIT – cross country track, avoiding Carcaillot Farm corner to road S of Meaulte, thence to billets at MORLANCOURT. Arrived 7-30 pm. Weather and roads very good. E.C.	
MORLANCOURT.	2-8-16.		Inspection at 1.45 pm by G.O.C. 35th Div: NE of Church who congratulated Brigade on recent work. Day spent in billets. E.C.	
			Baths 1-pm – 3-30 pm in ANCRE. Bombing practice 7am – 10 am. E.C.	
DO.	3-8-16.		Training 7am. – 10 a.m. Bombing 7am – 10 am, Transport	
DO.	4-8-16		Bathing 1pm – 3-30 pm. Training 5pm – 7pm. left for new Area. E.C.	
Do and TRAIN	5-8-16.		Battn marched to MERICOURT 12-15 pm. Entrained 4 pm. Detrained at SALEUX 8pm. Marched 14 miles to LE MESGE, arriving 1-30 a.m. Billets good. Transport had arrived 7-30 pm. Weather & roads good. Men tired after heavy work lately & the march. E.C.	
LE MESGE	6-8-16.		Day spent in billets cleaning up. Officers reconnoitred training grounds. Draft of 135 men arrived 10-30 pm. E.C.	
Do	7-8-16.		Battn training 6am – 10 am. on area F near RIENCOURT. 5pm – 7pm. Officers training under C.O. (Staff ride.) Range opened. Bombing 6am – 10am Coy training & bathing 5pm – 7pm. Weather & roads good. Canteen opened. E.C.	
Do.	8-8-16		Orders received that DIVISION will move back to 13th Corps Area on 9th & 10th. Transport to move on 9th. – Training 6 am – 10 am, Area E. near RIENCOURT. Coy training 5pm – 7pm. Officers had Lewis Gun instruction 5-6 pm. E.C.	
Do.	9-8-16		Transport left at 5 a.m. Day spent in billets. Weather good. Very hot. Men bathed. E.C.	
Do and Train.	10-8-16		Battn left LE MESGE at 5-15 pm. Entrained at HANGEST at 7pm. Train did not leave till 10 pm. Arrived MERICOURT 1-15 am. Battn reached billets at MORLANCOURT 3-15 am. 11-8-16. A draft of 49 reinforcements picked up at MERICOURT and marched with the Battn to billets. E.C.	

2449 Wt. W14957/M90 750,000 1/16 J.B.C. & A. Forms/C.2118/12.

Army Form C. 2118.

Instructions regarding War Diaries and Intelligence Summaries are contained in F. S. Regs., Part II. and the Staff Manual respectively. Title Pages will be prepared in manuscript.

WAR DIARY
or
INTELLIGENCE SUMMARY
(Erase heading not required.)

Place	Date	Hour	Summary of Events and Information	Remarks and references to Appendices
MORLANCOURT	11-8-16.		Reinforcements to number of 39 arrived. Day spent in billets – cleaning up and preparing for further movement. Weather very good, but very hot. E.L.	
DO.	12-8-16.		Coy training during the morning W+X Coys, 9 am-12 noon. Y+Z Coys, 6 am - 9 am. [illegible] demonstration The men were paid. Weather still good but very warm. Roads good E.L.	
DO.	13-8-16		Church Parade 9 am. Battn training 4 pm - 6 pm Weather good. Roads good E.L.	
DO.			Medical Officers report for week ending 12-8-16. "No special work to report. In billets occupied during the week fly proof latrines existed in 60% of the places. A few extra were erected. A new form of Fly trap arrived in sufficient numbers from ADMS to supply 2 per Coy. They have proved efficient, but more are needed to cope with the number of flies." A.A. Watson MO 1/c 17th West Yorks Regt	
DO.	14-8-16		Training 8 am - 10 am under Coy arrangements. Bathing 11 am - 1 30 pm. Battn training in attack 4-30 pm - 7 30 pm. Weather changed. Heavy rain in afternoon. Training had to be stopped. Training ground at BOIS DES TAILLES.	
DO.	15-8-16		Orders received to move on 16th to SAND PIT Valley. E18 a F19 a Sheet 62 D NE. Battn training 4-30 - 6 30 pm. Coy training 8 a.m - 10 a.m. Bathing at mid day E.L.	
Do to SAND PIT Valley	16-8-16		Battn left MORLANCOURT 10·35 a.m and marched via BRAY-CORBIE road, BRAY DIVERSION (E.14) to SAND PIT Valley, arriving 2 pm. Weather good, but roads dusty and hot. Rest of day spent in settling into Camp. E.L.	
SAND PIT VALLEY	17-8-16		Coy training in morning and afternoon. OC Coys went to inspect Battn training ground in afternoon. Weather good. E.L.	
DO	18-8-16		Battn training in attack 9 am - 12 noon. Bathing 7 am - 8 am. Coy training 5-30 - 6-30 pm. Demonstration by R.E. at 6 pm on making of T heads. Some rain weather breaking up. E.L.	

2449 Wt. W14957/M90 750,000 1/16 J.B.C. & A. Forms/C.2118/12.

Army Form. C. 2118.

WAR DIARY
or
INTELLIGENCE SUMMARY
(Erase heading not required.)

Instructions regarding War Diaries and Intelligence Summaries are contained in F. S. Regs., Part II. and the Staff Manual respectively. Title Pages will be prepared in manuscript.

Place	Date	Hour	Summary of Events and Information	Remarks and references to Appendices
SAND PIT Valley	19-8-16		Training in morning had to be abandoned owing to rain. Practice in attack had been arranged from 6am - 9 am. - Camp rearranged in afternoon. Football match V 18th H.L.I at 5-30 pm a good game. Battn lost 2-3. Orders received to move early tomorrow morning to S of Minden Post. (F18.c 3.3) Much rain during the day. G.L.	
Do and Contour Wood Camp. F.24.c.	20-8-16		Battn marched to Bivouac at about F23 c. starting 8-50am. Settled into camp by 11.30am. weather good G.L.	
	~~21-8-16~~		Medical Officer's Report for week ending 19-8-16 "47 fly proof latrines were fixed on day of arrival at Sand Pit Valley for Officers. Men had to use trench latrines owing to lack of material. These were dug deep, and earth & lime scattered in at frequent intervals. Medical work carried on as usual, the most notable feature of the sick parades being the increased number of cases of diarrhoea usually accompanied by abdominal pain. All yielded to treatment & none were evacuated. 17 cases evacuated from the Battn, & 7 from 106 MG Coy. A.A. Watson MO i/c 17th W Yorks R." E.P.	
Do	21-8-16		Company training in morning & afternoon. Wire, picks & shovels, water cans, etc received. These were divided up to take into trenches. A.S.T.	
do	22-8-16		Training in ~~[illegible]~~ camp. A.S.T.	
Silesia Trench	23-8-16		Moved up to Silesia trench. Arrived about 9.15 p.m. Stayed the night here. A.S.T.	
Silesia Trench	24-8-16		Received orders at 6.A.M. to relieve 19th D.L.I in front line by 12 noon, "W" & "Y" Companies to occupy Lonely & Bantam trenches; "Z" Coy Assembly trench & "X" Coy reserve trench. Left Silesia trench at 7.30 A.M. At arriving at the Briqueterie - Maricourt road we were informed that relief could not take place in daylight. "Y" Coy A.S.T.	

2449 Wt. W14957/M90 750,000 1/16 J.B.C. & A. Forms/C.2118/12.

Instructions regarding War Diaries and Intelligence Summaries are contained in F. S. Regs., Part II. and the Staff Manual respectively. Title Pages will be prepared in manuscript.

WAR DIARY
or
INTELLIGENCE SUMMARY

(Erase heading not required.)

Army Form C. 2118.

Place	Date	Hour	Summary of Events and Information	Remarks and references to Appendices
Silesia Trench & front line	24.8.16		"Y" Coy & 2 platoons of "W" Coy did not receive this message at the time & became detached. Remainder of "W", "Z" & "X" Coys moved back to Silesia trench. "Y" & 2 platoons of "W" occupied trench in Waltz Horn Valley. Batt moved up to front line at 9 p.m. AST.	
Front line	25.8.16		Relieved the 19th D.L.I. in Lonely, Bantam, assembly & res. trenches. Relief complete by 1.30 A.M. All trenches shelled heavily at 6 A.M. Fairly quiet during day. Received notice at 6 p.m. that Germans were likely to attack south of Guillemont. Intense bombardment by enemy started at 8 p.m. S.O.S signal sent up from our front line. Our bombardment became intense. Matters quietened down at 10 p.m. No attack on Battalion front. Slight shelling during remainder of night. AST	
do	26.8.16		Fairly quiet except for short period during the afternoon. Improved communicating trenches, also front line, assembly & reserve trenches. AST.	
do	27.8.16		Orders received that 1st Devons would relieve us at 11 p.m. Fairly quiet during day. Considerable bombardment between 10 p.m. & 11 p.m. "W" Coy relieved at midnight – other companies in turn relief being complete at 1.45 A.M. on 28/8/16. AST.	
Happy Valley	28.8.16		Marched to Happy Valley. Weather very bad. Everyone wet through. Four tents allotted to each company. Remainder of men made bivouacs. Arrived Happy Valley 7 A.M. AST	
	29.8.16		Company Training, Cleaning equipment etc. AST	

2449 Wt. W14957/M90 750,000 1/16 J.B.C. & A. Forms/C.2118/12.

Army Form C. 2118

WAR DIARY
or
INTELLIGENCE SUMMARY
(Erase heading not required.)

Instructions regarding War Diaries and Intelligence Summaries are contained in F. S. Regs., Part II. and the Staff Manual respectively. Title Pages will be prepared in manuscript.

Place	Date	Hour	Summary of Events and Information	Remarks and references to Appendices
Happy Valley & train	30.8.16		Experienced very bad weather. Neir bivouacs very little use. Company training. Left Happy Valley & marched via BRAY-ALBERT RD, BRAY DIVERSION & BRAY-CORBIE RD to HEILLY. Entrained here & detrained FIENVILLERS-CANDAS. Marched to BERNAVILLE a.s.t.	
Bernaville & Sus St Leger	31.8.16		Marched to SUS-ST-LEGER via DOULLENS & LUCHEUX. New drafts inspected by A.G. en route. Arrived at Sus St-LEGER 7 pm. a.s.t.	

1875 Wt. W593/826 1,000,000 4/15 J.B.C. & A. A.D.S.S./Forms/C. 2118.

Instructions regarding War Diaries and Intelligence Summaries are contained in F. S. Regs., Part II. and the Staff Manual respectively. Title pages will be prepared in manuscript.

WAR DIARY
or
INTELLIGENCE SUMMARY.
(Erase heading not required.)

17th W. Yorkshire Regt

Army Form C. 2118.

Vol 8

Place	Date	Hour	Summary of Events and Information	Remarks and references to Appendices
SUS ST LEGER	1.9.16		Rifle inspection & foot inspection. A.S.T.	
do & HAUTEVILLE	2.9.16		Left SUS ST LEGER at 2 pm for HAUTEVILLE. Arrived HAUTEVILLE 5.30 pm. A.S.T.	
			Medical Officer's report for week ending Sep 2/16 "During early part of week three officers & several "men were evacuated for diarrhoea & colic. The "number of cases of diarrhoea has been on the increase "Sanitary arrangements previously made in all our "billets. They are satisfactory. (Sd) A A Watson M.O. i/c 17th West Yorks". A.S.T.	
do	3.9.16		Company training. A.S.T.	
do	4.9.16		Inspection of Batt. by C.O. A.S.T.	
do	5.9.16			
DUISANS			Batt marched to DUISANS via LATTRE & HABARCQ arrived DUISANS at 1 pm.	

T2131. Wt. W708-776. 500000. 4/15. Sir J. C. & S.

Instructions regarding War Diaries and Intelligence Summaries are contained in F. S. Regs., Part II. and the Staff Manual respectively. Title Pages will be prepared in manuscript.

WAR DIARY
or
INTELLIGENCE SUMMARY
(Erase heading not required.)

Army Form C. 2118

Place	Date	Hour	Summary of Events and Information	Remarks and references to Appendices
Duisans	6/9/16		Company training. Received orders to go into K1 sector ARRAS on morning of the ~~tenth~~ then billetted in huts at DUISANS. Bathing for men at LOUEZ. A.S.T.	
	7.9.16		Company training morning & afternoon. Baths at LOUEZ. A.S.T.	
	8.9.16		Commanding Officer, Second in command & Coy Commdrs visited line in K1 sector. Company training for the men. A.S.T.	
ARRAS.	9.9.16.		Left DUISANS for ARRAS. Arrived ARRAS. 10.30 pm. Billetted there for the night. A.S.T.	
Trenches K1. Sector	10.9.16		Relieved Royal Scots in K.1 Sector. Relief complete mid-day. Thorough inspection of line made by officers & N.C.O's who found that lot of work was required to be done. ~~W~~ X.Y. & Z Coys in front line W. in reserve. W. Coy carried all meals, cooked at St Nicholas up to front line. Work of improving trenches begun. A.S.T.	
do	11.9.16.		Line fairly quiet except for Trench Mortars. Left Coy rather badly shelled by T.M's at night. Artillery retaliation was asked for. Patrols went out. Wire found to be weak in places. A.S.T.	

Instructions regarding War Diaries and Intelligence Summaries are contained in F. S. Regs., Part II. and the Staff Manual respectively. Title pages will be prepared in manuscript.

WAR DIARY
or
INTELLIGENCE SUMMARY.
(Erase heading not required.)

Army Form C. 2118.

Place	Date	Hour	Summary of Events and Information	Remarks and references to Appendices
Trenches K1 Sector	11.9.16		2nd Lt Martin wounded in eye. Evacuated. AST	
do	12.9.16		Work continued, but hindered by one company being occupied all day with carrying up meals. Duck boards laid, & revetting done. Also good deal of wiring AST	
do	13.9.16		Our trench mortars active. Enemy quieter than formerly. Work continued as before AST	
do	14.9.16		"Sniper's" posts started when Battalion went into line, completed. None in line when Batt. took over. Orders received to be prepared for a gas attack from our line K2 Sector. All preparations made, dugouts made gasproof; men wore helmets in alert position. ~~Att~~ Discharge of gas did not take place apparently owing to unfavourable wind.	
do	~~15.9.16~~		General Penney visited line & presented Ptes Vero & Marshall with ribbon of Military Medal AST	

T.134. Wt. W798-776. 500000. 4/15. Sir J. C. & S.

Instructions regarding War Diaries and Intelligence Summaries are contained in F. S. Regs., Part II. and the Staff Manual respectively. Title pages will be prepared in manuscript.

WAR DIARY
or
INTELLIGENCE SUMMARY.
(Erase heading not required.)

Army Form C. 2118.

Place	Date	Hour	Summary of Events and Information	Remarks and references to Appendices
Trenches K1 Sector	15.9.16		Quiet day. Work continued in trenches. AST.	
	16.9.16		Relieved by 17th Royal Scots. Relief Complete 11 AM. W. Coy took up support line at Roclincourt & "Z" coy also went into support two platoons at Roclincourt one platoon at observatory fort & one platoon at Thelus redoubt. Y Company billetted at St Nicholas & X Coy in ARRAS. Medical Officers Report for week ending 16/9/16. "Medical arrangements satisfactory. Stretcher cases carried from trenches to aid post by Regimental Stretcher bearers & from aid post to adv. dressing station by Stretcher bearers attached to aid post from Fld. Amb. Number of wounded evacuated during 6 days – 20. Two were severely wounded. Sick were brought to aid post daily. Sanitary arrangements good. Latrine tins emptied at night & contents buried behind trenches. A.A. Watson M.O. i/c 17th West Yorks." AST.	

T.134. Wt. W708-776. 500000. 4/15. Sir J. C. & S.

Army Form C. 2118.

Instructions regarding War Diaries and Intelligence Summaries are contained in F. S. Regs., Part II. and the Staff Manual respectively. Title pages will be prepared in manuscript.

WAR DIARY
or
INTELLIGENCE SUMMARY.
(Erase heading not required.)

Place	Date	Hour	Summary of Events and Information	Remarks and references to Appendices
ARRAS. ROCLINCOURT St NICHOLAS	17/9/16 18.9.16 19/9/16 20/9/16 21/9.16		Bombing classes - 8 men per Coy - were held daily at St Nicholas, & men attending were billetted with Y Coy. Companies were used daily as carrying parties & working parties were also provided, by Z Coy for R.E's in connection with Roclincourt defences	ASt
Trenches K1 Sector	22.9.16		Relieved the 17th Royal Scots in K1 Sector. Relief complete at 11 AM. Patrols went out at night & Lewis Guns fired on gaps in enemy wire. Good shooting by our Stokes. Enemy T.M's very active between 4 pm & 7 pm. Blew in about 20 yds of front line trench 108 & part of New St. Shells appeared to be "Rumjars". Wiring done from front line to Kent Crater. Duckboards laid in front line. Revetting done. ASt	
do	23.9.16		Our T.M's carried out wire cutting operations. Enemy T.M's active during afternoon. Many "duds" came over. Lewis Gunners were sniped at during night when guns were firing. Enemy placed sentries near their gaps in wire	ASt

T.131. Wt. W798-776. 500000. 4/15. Sir J. C. & S.

Instructions regarding War Diaries and Intelligence Summaries are contained in F. S. Regs., Part II. and the Staff Manual respectively. Title pages will be prepared in manuscript.

WAR DIARY
or
INTELLIGENCE SUMMARY.
(Erase heading not required.)

Army Form C. 2118.

Place	Date	Hour	Summary of Events and Information	Remarks and references to Appendices
Trenches K.1. Sector	23.9.16		Medical officer's report for week ending 23.9.16. Sanitary arrangements in ARRAS were carried out according to Town regulations. Company's outside town had to carry rubbish to incinerator. In some places new fly proof latrines were supplied by the Batt. As two Coys were in trenches sick parade was small. Sick of two Coys referred to were attended to by M.O. at aid post. Ten men were evacuated during the week. A A Watson M.O. i/c 17th West Yorks	
			A.A.T.	

Instructions regarding War Diaries and Intelligence Summaries are contained in F. S. Regs., Part II. and the Staff Manual respectively. Title pages will be prepared in manuscript.

WAR DIARY
or
INTELLIGENCE SUMMARY.
(Erase heading not required.)

Army Form C. 2118.

Place	Date	Hour	Summary of Events and Information	Remarks and references to Appendices
Trenches K1 Sector	24.9.16		Revetting work, laying of duckboards, & wiring done. Six patrols went out at night. Our Stokes fired 63 rounds. Enemy T.M's active, shells dropping near our Stokes emplacements. During the day two motor transports & a motor car went along road from H.8.C 10.1 to ATHIES also other transport between 5pm & 7pm. Ast	
do	25.9.16		Between 5pm & 7pm enemy sent over about 50 light T.M's which fell behind trenches 108-111. No damage done. Practically no M.G or rifle fire at night. Enemy wiring party dispersed by our L.G. & rifle fire. Good deal of transport seen behind enemy lines. Harvesting continued. No movements noticed in enemy front line. Our trenches considerably improved. Bombs overhauled. Ast.	
do.	26.9.16		Our Stokes damaged enemy parapet opposite Kent Crater. Enemy T.M's which were fairly active did no damage. Sentries in centre Coy are confident	

T.2134. Wt. W708-776. 500000. 4/15. Sir J. C. & S.

Instructions regarding War Diaries and Intelligence Summaries are contained in F. S. Regs., Part II. and the Staff Manual respectively. Title pages will be prepared in manuscript.

WAR DIARY
or
INTELLIGENCE SUMMARY.
(Erase heading not required.)

Army Form C. 2118.

Place	Date	Hour	Summary of Events and Information	Remarks and references to Appendices
Trenches K1 Sector	26.9.16		that they heard sounds of digging under them a little to the right of Kick Crater. Good deal of revetting work was done & parapets were also strengthened. Number of "gooseberries" were made. A.S.T.	
do	27.9.16		Our field guns got some direct hits on enemy front line. Our Stokes also fired. There was no retaliation. Later, enemy retaliated on our Stokes. Rifle fire rather more active than usual during night. An enemy patrol was dispersed by our Lewis Guns. There was good deal of enemy movement about FARBUS Wood. Periscopes seen in various parts of enemy line. Our snipers claim a victim. A.S.T.	
do & ARRAS	28.9.16		Relieved by ~~Ro~~ 17th Royal Scots. Relief complete 10.30 am. Battalion marched to billets in ARRAS. Orders to move to ~~B~~ DUISANS at night ~~so~~ were cancelled during the day. Batt. remained at ARRAS. A.S.T.	

Instructions regarding War Diaries and Intelligence Summaries are contained in F. S. Regs., Part II. and the Staff Manual respectively. Title pages will be prepared in manuscript.

WAR DIARY
or
INTELLIGENCE SUMMARY.
(Erase heading not required.)

Army Form C. 2118.

Place	Date	Hour	Summary of Events and Information	Remarks and references to Appendices
ARRAS	29.9.16		Inspections were carried out by Companies in billets. Arming drill & physical drill was also carried out under cover. A.S.T.	
do	30.9.16		Company training carried on as far as possible under cover. Orders were received for carrying up gas cylinders to the line (104th Bde front) A.S.T.	
			Medical officer's report for week ending 30/9/16. Sanitary work in trenches carried out as usual. Boxes in one latrine were replaced by more satisfactory ones. During latter part of week much work was done in ARRAS by Sanitary squad in clearing away accumulation of rubbish help being received from Sanitary officer. Latrine refuse & all wet refuse is removed by cart at night. Dry refuse is placed in sandbags & taken away on handcart to the incinerator	
			A.A. Walton M O i/c 17 West Yorks.	
			A.S.T.	

T.134. Wt. W708–776. 500000. 4/15. Sir J. C. & S.

17th W Yorks

17th W. Yorks R

VOL 9

WAR DIARY
or
INTELLIGENCE SUMMARY.
(Erase heading not required.)

Army Form C. 2118.

Instructions regarding War Diaries and Intelligence Summaries are contained in F. S. Regs., Part II. and the Staff Manual respectively. Title pages will be prepared in manuscript.

Place	Date	Hour	Summary of Events and Information	Remarks and references to Appendices
ARRAS	1.10.16		Arrangements made for carrying up gas cylinders to line (104th Bde front). Fifteen parties, each party consisting of 1 officer, 2 N.C.O's & 30 men were detailed. First party left dump at DOUAI 8.35 pm. & last party 10.30 pm. First party arrived back in billets soon after eleven pm & last party about 1.30 A.M. (2/10/16). A.S.T.	
do	2.10.16		Company training as far as possible. Lewis Gun lectures by L.G. sergeant. Carrying parties for gas cylinders accomplished work similar to previous evening. A.S.T.	
do	3.10.16 } 4.10.16 }		Company training & carrying parties for gas cylinders. A.S.T.	
do K1 Sector	5.10.16		Left billets in ARRAS for K.1 Sector. First company started [illegible] pm. Relief complete 4 pm. Work of clearing New St & Victoria St started & completed. Fire steps built in Trenches 108 & 111. ~~Orders received to prepare for gas attack on enemy from our left & right. Received code word~~ last	

Instructions regarding War Diaries and Intelligence Summaries are contained in F. S. Regs., Part II. and the Staff Manual respectively. Title pages will be prepared in manuscript.

WAR DIARY
or
INTELLIGENCE SUMMARY.

(Erase heading not required.)

Army Form C. 2118.

Place	Date	Hour	Summary of Events and Information	Remarks and references to Appendices
R1.	5.10.16		~~twice that attack discharge wd take place, but cancellation came on each occasion.~~ A.S.T.	
do	6.10.16		Enemy T.M's very active during afternoon & evening & our No 3 gun emplacement was hit. Our Stokes retaliated. Movement of men & transport seen near ATHIES. Code word came that gas discharge wd take place on our left & right, but cancellation came. Work was interfered with on this account. New Latrines however were built & trenches were strengthened.	
do	7.10.16		Four patrols went out during the night, but nothing unusual was seen. L Guns fired on gaps in enemy wire. Two of our men wounded by shell fire. Code word for gas discharge received again, but it was cancelled. Considerable amount of work was done in revetting & relaying duck boards.	
~~do~~	~~8.10.16~~		~~Code word for gas again received, zero time being 8.45 pm during the operations our Stokes fired 104 rounds~~ A.S.T.	

Instructions regarding War Diaries and Intelligence Summaries are contained in F. S. Regs., Part II. and the Staff Manual respectively. Title Pages will be prepared in manuscript.

WAR DIARY
or
INTELLIGENCE SUMMARY
(Erase heading not required.)

Army Form C. 2118

Place	Date	Hour	Summary of Events and Information	Remarks and references to Appendices
K 1.	7/10/16		Medical Officer's Report for week ending 7/10/16. Medical work carried on as usual in ARRAS & in trenches Larger number of men than usual among those reporting sick have been suffering from feverish conditions. Much work was done in ARRAS removing rubbish from billets, while latrine accommodation in men's quarters was increased by 4 fly proof latrines & necessary roofing. In trenches a good start was made in work of supplying screens, roofs & paper boxes to all existing latrines, & also soak pits for urine tins. A. A Watson. M.O. i/c 17th West-Yorks Regt	
K 1.	8.10.16		Code word for gas again received zero hour being 8.45 pm. During the operations our Stokes fired 149 rounds; rifle grenades fired 68, 8 Lewis Guns fired about 3,500 rounds. 60 smoke bombs were thrown from Kite Crater. Gas discharged on our flanks. Our front line was thinned out & all men wore gas helmets at "Gas Alert" position. No one in our line felt ~~the~~ any effects of gas discharged. Apart from a disused trench little damage was done by enemy retaliation. Enemy sent many green red & white lights up after zero	A.A.T.

1875 Wt. W593/826 1,000,000 4/15 J.B.C. & A. A.D.S.S./Forms/C. 2118.

Instructions regarding War Diaries and Intelligence Summaries are contained in F. S. Regs., Part II. and the Staff Manual respectively. Title Pages will be prepared in manuscript.

WAR DIARY
or
INTELLIGENCE SUMMARY
(Erase heading not required.)

Army Form C. 2118

Place	Date	Hour	Summary of Events and Information	Remarks and references to Appendices
K1	8.10.16		Work done in line included clearing trenches where they had fallen in; revetting; re-laying of trench boards; carrying parties for T.M ammunition. Ast	
K.1	9.10.16		A hostile field gun was observed to be firing at 8.15 pm on the Division on our left from a bearing 23° East of TRUE NORTH from the centre Coy H.Q. It appeared to be about 1,000 yds away. Two German O.P's appeared to be at G 6 A 7.7 & G 6 A 7.6. Enemy sent up green & red lights during a sharp artillery & bombing operation. We did 35 yds of wiring from GRIDIRON LANE to centre of 103. Work was hampered owing to bright moon. 30 Gooseberries placed in front of 108. Trench revetting etc. carried on as usual. We dispersed several hostile wiring parties during the night. Ast	
K.1.	10.10.16		Our artillery stopped hostile trench mortars about 4.30 pm. We suffered considerable damage however. Seven men were killed & two wounded, all in vicinity of our Stokes emplacements. One heavy T.M. fell above entrance of 30 ft dug-out in VICTORIA St. The entrance was completely demolished & filled in to within 5 feet of the bottom. One Lewis Gun was destroyed by T.M. Work of clearing trenches blown in took considerable time, & much work was ~~of~~ done in repairing them. Latrine accommodation [illegible]. Sniper claimed a victim at G 6 C 7.4. Enemy placed a large periscope	

Instructions regarding War Diaries and Intelligence Summaries are contained in F. S. Regs., Part II. and the Staff Manual respectively. Title Pages will be prepared in manuscript.

WAR DIARY
or
INTELLIGENCE SUMMARY
(Erase heading not required.)

Army Form C. 2118

Place	Date	Hour	Summary of Events and Information	Remarks and references to Appendices
K1	10.10.16		opposite KENT Crater. 18 inches wide & 9" high. It was covered at intervals by a brown cloth. It was not fired at yesterday as many Germans were seen by its reflection during the day. An officer was seen looking through it. ~~[illegible]~~ continually passed the spot wearing the usual grey uniform with red braid on collars & shoulder straps & a silver badge on shoulder strap. A sniper fired at periscope 4 times this morning & claims to have hit it each time. It was taken down after the 4th shot. A.S.T.	
K1 ARRAS & St Nicholas	11.10.16		Batt. was relieved by the 17th Royal Scots. Relief complete 10.15 AM. One company went to billets in ARRAS, one to billets in St NICHOLAS; one to trenches at ROCLINCOURT; two platoons of the 4th Coy to trenches at ROCLINCOURT; one platoon to THELUS Redoubt & one platoon to OBSERVATORY Fort. A.S.T.	
ARRAS St Nicholas & K1.	12.10.16		Bombing Class – 8 men per Coy, & Lewis Gun Class – 2 officers & 16 O.R. held at St NICHOLAS. "Z" Coy found working party of 30 men for T.M. ammunition carrying. "W" Coy also found 12 men for the same purpose. Baths allotted to the Batt. A.S.T.	
do	13.10.16		Bombing & L.G ~~[illegible]~~ classes continued. Remainder ~~available~~ in ARRAS & St NICHOLAS underwent company training. A.S.T.	

1875 Wt. W593/826 1,000,000 4/15 J.B.C. & A. A.D.S.S./Forms/C. 2118.

Instructions regarding War Diaries and Intelligence Summaries are contained in F. S. Regs., Part II. and the Staff Manual respectively. Title Pages will be prepared in manuscript.

WAR DIARY
or
INTELLIGENCE SUMMARY
(Erase heading not required.)

Army Form C. 2118

Place	Date	Hour	Summary of Events and Information	Remarks and references to Appendices
ARRAS St Nicholas K1	14.10.16		Bombing & Lewis Gun classes. Bathing at Rue de LILLE baths. Working parties as on 12/10/16 Adjt.	
	~~[illegible]~~ ~~[illegible]~~		M.O's report for week ending 14/10/16. Most of latrines in trenches supplied with roofs & screens. During period out of line endeavours were made to keep floors of men's billets cleaner. New tins grease supplied. Medical work as usual. Adjt. A.A. Watson. Lt. O/C 17th West Yorks.	
do	15.10.16 16.10.16		Working parties for carrying ~~[illegible]~~ Stokes Ammunition up to the line, also parties for R.E. Bombing & Lewis Gun classes. Baths. Remainder of men did company training as far as practicable Adjt.	
K1	17.10.16		Battn relieved the 17th Royal Scots in K1 Sector. Relief complete at 12.7 pm. During the afternoon two light T.M's were put into VICTORIA ST. by enemy. Support & works lines were shelled but no damage was done. Enemy quiet at night. Our L.G's fired on gaps in enemy wire. Four patrols went out. Heavy rain interfered with their work. During the afternoon a German was seen at G.6.b.7.7. He was fired on & was seen to fall. Observation balloon behind FARBUS WOOD went up & stayed in the air for 30 minutes. Work done included revetting, laying of duck boards, wiring Adjt.	
K1.	18.10.16		Retaliation ~~was~~ by Artillery was called for by left Coy at 3.30 pm & this quietened enemy T.M's for a time. Our Artillery fired on Pope's Nose during the afternoon.	

1875 Wt. W593/826 1,000,000 4/15 J.B.C. & A. A.D.S.S./Forms/C. 2118.

Army Form C. 2118

Instructions regarding War Diaries and Intelligence Summaries are contained in F. S. Regs., Part II. and the Staff Manual respectively. Title Pages will be prepared in manuscript.

WAR DIARY
or
INTELLIGENCE SUMMARY
(Erase heading not required.)

Place	Date	Hour	Summary of Events and Information	Remarks and references to Appendices
K 1	18.10.16		Enemy retaliated on Kick Crater & sap leading to it. He also fired at intervals of 3 to 5 minutes on ~~[illegible]~~ ROCLINCOURT & SUNDAY AV. One shell burst in trench in front of OBSERVATORY FORT. Whizbangs were sent over ranging from support line to front line. In the morning enemy T.M's were active especially on left sub-sector where some damage was done to trenches. Hostile M.G. believed to be firing from POPE'S NOSE traversed our front line at night. Sniper in KATIE CRATER heard stakes being driven in old French trench at 9 AM. Men were seen working. A patrol was fired on from HUN front line. One green light was sent up on our left. There were no other coloured lights. Work done. Duck boards laid, recesses made for S.A.A. Sentry post repaired, wire strengthened on left of KATIE CRATER., revetting, trench deepened in E work. New battle emplacement built in 102 by M.G's. A.S.T.	
K 1	19.10.16		Light was bad for observation. Smoke was seen to ascend from road at B.8 d 2.4 in the morning. German sentry wearing cap with red band was seen. Patrols reported no signs of working parties or enemy patrols. Enemy was comparatively quiet, though T.M's were active now & again. Our Stokes fired 40 rounds, & we also fired 70 or 80 rifle grenades. Work was continued in the line. A.S.T.	

1875 Wt. W593/826 1,000,000 4/15 J.B.C. & A. A.D.S.S./Forms/C. 2118.

Instructions regarding War Diaries and Intelligence Summaries are contained in F. S. Regs., Part II. and the Staff Manual respectively. Title Pages will be prepared in manuscript.

WAR DIARY
or
INTELLIGENCE SUMMARY

(Erase heading not required.)

Army Form C. 2118

Place	Date	Hour	Summary of Events and Information	Remarks and references to Appendices
K1	20.10.16		Our field guns fired on the POPE'S Nose during the afternoon, & also on enemy's line opposite 110. There were 12 direct hits. Enemy sent 10 rum jars over 108 at 3.30 pm. One fell in our trench. Our wire was cut by enemy shells in front of 103 & N of KATIE CRATER. One of our aeroplanes was brought down in the afternoon near B27 d 2.4. It descended slowly. Enemy was seen removing it. The balloon near FARBUS WOOD was up all night. A light was observed in it, but no signalling was noticed. An unusually large amount of Transport was heard behind German line from 6 pm to 9 pm. Much smoke was seen in enemy support line. Considerable clashing of metal was heard opposite KITE CRATER. Patrol went out to investigate & reported that enemy was driving in stakes. In the morning a man was seen waving a white flag about B4.d7.3. Work done. Clearing away falls, wiring, revetting, laying duckboards, shelter built. Parapet rebuilt in places. A.S.T.	
K1.	21.10.16		Patrols reported enemy wire very strong. Enemy unusually quiet all night. T M's very active in morning & afternoon. Our trenches blown in in 8 places. Artillery quiet. Work done similar to that done on 20/10/16. A.S.T.	

1875 Wt. W593/826 1,000,000 4/15 J.B.C. & A. A.D.S.S./Forms/C. 2118.

Army Form C. 2118

Instructions regarding War Diaries and Intelligence Summaries are contained in F. S. Regs., Part II. and the Staff Manual respectively. Title Pages will be prepared in manuscript.

WAR DIARY
or
INTELLIGENCE SUMMARY
(Erase heading not required.)

Place	Date	Hour	Summary of Events and Information	Remarks and references to Appendices
K1	21.10.16		M.O's report for week ending 21/10/16. Chest complaints were more numerous than usual, probably owing to wet weather. Much work was done in keeping latrines in line in order. About half the soakage pits were re-placed by waterproof oil drums. Another cookhouse was whitewashed A.A. Watson M.O. i/c 17th West Yorks. A.S.T.	
K1	22.10.16		Our stokes fired 87 rounds & T.M's 25 rounds. L.G's fired in gaps in enemy's wire, & 50 rifle grenades were fired. Wiring party was dispersed by our L.G's. Field guns fired 15 rounds at 7.30 pm in retaliation to enemy T.M's which were very active, firing several hundred rounds during day. These T.M's are of heavy calibre & have long range. Left Coy Sgt-Major killed by T.M. & Centre Coy Commander wounded. Two privates were also killed. About 4.30 pm one of our aeroplanes was brought down behind German line about B.19.c.6.5. Rifle fire was opened on it by our troops & Artillery were acquainted. A Lewis Gun was trained on it pending the arrival of a Vickers. Many of the enemy gathered round the plane, & they were fired on with shrapnel. Much work was done in our line. A.S.T.	

1875 Wt. W593/826 1,000,000 4/15 J.B.C. & A. A.D.S.S./Forms/C. 2118.

Army Form C. 2118

Instructions regarding War Diaries and Intelligence Summaries are contained in F. S. Regs., Part II. and the Staff Manual respectively. Title Pages will be prepared in manuscript.

WAR DIARY
or
INTELLIGENCE SUMMARY
(Erase heading not required.)

Place	Date	Hour	Summary of Events and Information	Remarks and references to Appendices
K1 & ARRAS	23.10.16		Battalion was relieved by 17th Royal Scots. Relief complete 10.45 Am. Men proceeded to billets in ARRAS where they were in Div. Res. A working party of 50 men was provided at night for R.E. ast	
ARRAS	24.10.16		Two companies bathed. All men available for working parties were used during either the day or night. ast	
do	25.10.16 / 26.10.16		Every available man was used for working parties – carrying stokes & T.M. ammunition; work on front line K1 sector, etc. ast	
do	27.10.16		Day working parties finished at noon. Battalion was engaged during the night in carrying up gas cylinders to the 104th Bde front. ast	
~~do~~	~~28.10.16~~		~~[illegible]~~	
do	28.10.16		Carrying of gas cylinders begun on night of 27/10/16 finished about 2 A.M. Men rested & cleaned up during the remainder of the day. ast	
			Medical Report for week ending 28/10/16. During most of the week we were in ARRAS & did a good deal of work to improve latrines & washing places. Medical work continued as usual. A larger percentage complained of chest-trouble & rheumatics. P. A. Watson M.O. i/c 14th West Yorks.	
			a.d.T.	

1875 Wt. W593/826 1,000,000 4/15 J.B.C. & A. A.D.S.S./Forms/C. 2118.

Instructions regarding War Diaries and Intelligence Summaries are contained in F. S. Regs., Part II. and the Staff Manual respectively. Title Pages will be prepared in manuscript.

WAR DIARY
or
INTELLIGENCE SUMMARY
(Erase heading not required.)

Army Form C. 2118

Place	Date	Hour	Summary of Events and Information	Remarks and references to Appendices
~~29~~ ARRAS & K1.	29.10.16		Battn relieved 17th Royal Scots in K1 Sector. Relief complete 10.45 Am. Our Stokes & Medium T.M's made good shooting on enemy's parapet during morning & evening. At night Lewis guns fired about 2600 rounds at gaps in enemy's wire. Our artillery silenced enemy T.M's during the afternoon. Parties of men were seen going toward FARBUS WOOD carrying picks & shovels. Patrols S.E. of Kent-Crater reported sounds of working in German lines; otherwise everything was quiet. Work done in our line ~~ex~~ included repairing trenches, laying duck boards, wiring, deepening trenches, etc. A.S.T.	
~~do~~ K1	30/10/16		At 4 AM a party of Germans were seen working at about H 9. This was reported to Artillery but no action was taken. A M.G emplacement & sniper's post suspected opposite Trench 114. Officer's patrol inspected wire at place of entry for proposed raid & reported considerable amount of low wire in front of main wire. Enemy T.M's were active but not much damage was done. Our T.M's & Stokes retaliated, & our artillery also fired with good effect. A.S.T.	
do	31st 10.16		Our artillery fired on German support line behind G 6. c & 9. with good results. Enemy searched with T.M's for our Vickers. No damage. At 7 pm several shells of large calibre burst near ROCLINCOURT. Much ~~of~~ work going on in enemy's front line presumably owing to damage done by wet. Officer's patrol reported sentry near place of entry for proposed raid. Bombs were thrown. Work done in our line; clearing falls, revetting & wiring. A.S.T.	

1875 Wt. W593/826 1,000,000 4/15 J.B.C. & A. A.D.S.S./Forms/C. 2118.

*Instructions regarding War Diaries and Intelligence Summaries are contained in F. S. Regs., Part II. and the Staff Manual respectively. Title Pages will be prepared in manuscript.

WAR DIARY
or
INTELLIGENCE SUMMARY
(Erase heading not required.)

17th West Yorks — Army Form C. 2118

November 1916.

Vol 10

Place	Date	Hour	Summary of Events and Information	Remarks and references to Appendices
K1	1·11·16		Light very bad. At 10·30 AM party of 20 men seen to leave trenches about H 28 & go into MONCHY. They returned shortly, & appeared to be carrying Trench Mortars. Enemy working hard on his front line. All our available men were occupied in clearing places blown in by enemy T.M's. Enemy appear to have very large number of T.M's. One very heavy one fires on right Coy front. Raid was arranged to take place tonight but owing to an unexpected strafe by Batt on our left — which brought forth very heavy strafe by the enemy. Raid was postponed. A.S.T.	
do	2·11·16		Hostile aeroplanes flew up & down our line during the afternoon & evening T.M's were very busy for several hours. Our centre Company front suffered very severe damages trenches 106 & 107 being practically levelled. The postponed raid was proceeded with. Patrols were sent out early & later in the evening two BANGALORE torpedoes were placed under wire under supervision of an officer. These were exploded electrically soon after 1 AM & two officers & 32 men entered the German line — 1 officer & 16 men going to the left & 1 off & 16 men to the right. Artillery formed a box barrage. The parties were in the line about 15 minutes & accounted for five or six Germans. One officer secured the shoulder strap from a German, & the regiment was identified as the 89th Grenadiers. All our men returned to our lines unhurt with the exception of one man who had a slight wound apparently caused by a small piece of shell. A.S.T.	

1875 Wt. W593/826 1,000,000 4/15 J.B.C. & A. A.D.S.S./Forms/C. 2118.

Instructions regarding War Diaries and Intelligence Summaries are contained in F. S. Regs., Part II. and the Staff Manual respectively. Title Pages will be prepared in manuscript.

WAR DIARY
or
INTELLIGENCE SUMMARY
(Erase heading not required.)

Army Form C. 2118

Place	Date	Hour	Summary of Events and Information	Remarks and references to Appendices
K 1.	3.11.16		Our Stokes & Mediums made good shooting on enemy front line & timber was hurled into the air from trenches opposite 108 & 110. The enemy was much quieter than usual. He appeared to be repairing his front line. We wired in front of trenches 106 + 107 & wiring was done along New St by a party from Bde reserve. A company of Northumberland Fusiliers worked on trenches 106 + 107 & did very good work clearing these trenches, NEW ST & CANNON ST. Cover of sorts was then made all the way along the front line & up to the post in Kick Crater. A company of Cheshire Regt on our right which had fallen back to its reserve line on 2nd inst. moved up again, & our right flank was again protected. The large T.M. of the enemy fired from a new position about G 6 c 10.8, which rather confirms suggestion that this T.M. is on trolley line. A.S.T.	
K 1 & Bde Res.	4.11.16		Battn relieved by the 17th Royal Scots. Relief complete abt 11.0 AM. One company billeted in St Nicholas; one took up works line (G.H.I.L works) in K 2; another went to trenches in ROCLINCOURT & another occupied THELUS REDOUBT, OBSERVATORY FORT & E & F works (K1). Company in St NICHOLAS provided working party of 1 officer & 40 men at night. A.S.T. Medical report for week ending 4.10.16. Sanitary police had a good deal of work repairing latrines damaged by trench mortars. Many of the men who reported sick had severe colds. A A Watson M.O. i/c 17th W. Yorks A.S.T.	

1875 Wt. W593/826 1,000,000 4/15 J.B.C. & A. A.D.S.S./Forms/C. 2118.

Instructions regarding War Diaries and Intelligence Summaries are contained in F. S. Regs., Part II. and the Staff Manual respectively. Title pages will be prepared in manuscript.

WAR DIARY
or
INTELLIGENCE SUMMARY.
(Erase heading not required.)

Army Form C. 2118.

Place	Date	Hour	Summary of Events and Information	Remarks and references to Appendices
K1 Bde Res.	5.11.16 to 9.11.16		Companies in the posts & works lines did considerable amount of work improving their positions. Owing to exceptionally heavy rains, there were many falls of trenches, & consequently work which wd otherwise have done was hampered considerably. The company in billets in St-NICHOLAS found working parties (generally with officers) to help in the work of clearing up the front line of K1. damaged very considerably by hostile fire & the heavy rains. They had baths at St-NICHOLAS, & the companies in posts etc bathed at ROCLINCOURT under Coy arrangements. A.S.T.	
K1	10.11.16		Relieved the Royal Scots. Relief complete by 12.50 pm. Our Stokes fired during the afternoon in counter offensive to enemy's whizz bangs & T.M's. Three enemy aeroplanes were fired on by our M.G's & A.A. Guns & machines were driven away. A patrol reported enemy wire very good in front of Pope's Nose. An enemy aeroplane could be heard flying over our lines at night. Work done. Reclaiming trenches clearing trenches & saps, draining & revetting. A.S.T.	

Army Form C. 2118

Instructions regarding War Diaries and Intelligence Summaries are contained in F. S. Regs., Part II. and the Staff Manual respectively. Title Pages will be prepared in manuscript.

WAR DIARY
or
INTELLIGENCE SUMMARY
(Erase heading not required.)

Place	Date	Hour	Summary of Events and Information	Remarks and references to Appendices
K1.	10.11.16		Medical Officer's report for week ending 10/11/16. Billets of men were clean & tidy. Latrines & cookhouses in good sanitary condition. Y Coy's billet had leaking roofs in places. The source of water supply was inspected & barbed wire was put round so as to prevent pollution of the spring. H. W. Heasman M.O i/c 14th West Yorks. A.S.T.	
do	11.11.16		Enemy sent over few whiz bangs during the day, & at night there was much more rifle fire than usual. About G 6. c 5.8 enemy has placed barbed wire along his parapet & has strengthened his wire along the whole front. Our troops did great deal of work building parapets, clearing trenches, revetting etc. A.S.T.	
do	12.11.16		Indications of much work in enemy's front line. Boards were seen above the parapet. Earth was also thrown up in many places. Our patrol at night reported enemy wire very thick. A sap previously made at G 6. c 5.8 was blocked up with knife rests. Artillery & T.M's fairly quiet. Owing to apparently to a man failing to warn sentry on our right, patrol was bombed by men of next Battn. No casualties. A.S.T.	
	13.11.16		Our Stokes retaliated to hostile fire from T.M's & an artillery fired at intervals during the day. Gunners fired very short at times, Howitzers being those concerned. One shell fell in KENT CRATER & two behind it. Sap to KICK CRATER was damaged also. Vickers Guns fired two at night. Night was bad & observation difficult. However a large working party of the enemy was seen digging trenches on sky line to right of FARBUS WOOD. Officer's patrol reported much talking & singing in enemy's lines, which seemed to indicate a relief. No hostile patrols seen. Work of clearing our line, revetting etc was carried on. A.S.T.	

1875 Wt. W593/826 1,000,000 4/15 J.B.C. & A. A.D.S.S./Forms/C. 2118.

Instructions regarding War Diaries and Intelligence Summaries are contained in F. S. Regs., Part II. and the Staff Manual respectively. Title Pages will be prepared in manuscript.

WAR DIARY
or
INTELLIGENCE SUMMARY
(Erase heading not required.)

Army Form C. 2118

Place	Date	Hour	Summary of Events and Information	Remarks and references to Appendices
K1	14.11.16		At 10 AM small parties of men were seen behind the NINE TREES & also behind the HAYSTACKS. Horse wagons were seen moving along road in front of FARBUS WOOD at 2 pm. At 1.30 AM one of our aeroplanes came over our lines & dropped two white lights about G 6 b 5.6. It proceeded over the German lines & returned about 4.30 am. Enemy artillery & T M's fairly quiet. Our guns registered on enemy's support line behind POPE'S NOSE. Support platoons of right & left coys practised counter attack across the open on the front line.	
do	15.11.16		Very quiet along our front all day & night. Heated argument was heard taking place in Hun line opposite KATIE CRATER. The word ~~Som~~ "SOMME" was frequently heard. Much work was done in our line. A.S.T.	
do & ARRAS	16.11.16		Relieved by ~~Roy~~ 17th Royal Scots. Relief complete 10.30 AM. Proceeded to billets in ARRAS. One company billeted in School for Blind Deaf & Dumb two under the Museum & one in the Granary. Reached billets between 12 noon & 1 pm. Working parties sent up to the front line later in the day. A.S.T.	
ARRAS	16.11.16		M.O's report for week ending Nov 16th 1916. Repairs carried out at RAMC dugout in Sunday Av. Latrines attended to & are now in good order. Water tanks at Thelus Redoubt satisfactory, & dugouts are in satisfactory condition. H.W. Heasman MO i/c 17th West Yorks. A.S.T.	
do	17.11.16 18.11.16 19.11.16 20.11.16 21.11.16		Battalion used for working parties. All available men out either day or night. An average of 50 men a day detailed to help on the work in front line K.1. ~~Two~~ Two parties of 20 each under an officer. Parties of men reported to R.E. for work under their supervision. 60 reported each night & 120 each morning. Other small parties were also detailed. Baths allotted to the Battn on two days, & all men bathed. A.S.T.	

1875 Wt. W593/826 1,000,000 4/15 J.B.C. & A. A.D.S.S./Forms/C. 2118.

Army Form C. 2118.

WAR DIARY
or
INTELLIGENCE SUMMARY
(Erase heading not required.)

Instructions regarding War Diaries and Intelligence Summaries are contained in F. S. Regs., Part II. and the Staff Manual respectively. Title Pages will be prepared in manuscript.

Place	Date	Hour	Summary of Events and Information	Remarks and references to Appendices
K1	22.11.16		Relieved 17th Royal Scots in K1. At 2 pm combined shoot by our artillery & T.M's was carried out, also Stokes Guns. The target was POPE'S NOSE. Shooting was good with the exception of Howitzers which dropped some shells short. There was little retaliation by the enemy. Lewis Guns fired at night paying particular attention to gaps reported by Royal Scots at G 6 a 7.9 in enemy's wire. Snipers' posts were reconstructed. Fresh earth has been thrown up behind enemy front line about G 6 a 8.2. Our troops did much work clearing trenches & revetting. Wiring was also done to right of Kent Crater. AST	
do	23.11.16		Suspected M.G. emplacement opposite Sap 109 A at G 6 a 65.85 was observed to be knocked in & part of concrete emplacement thrown on to parapet. Snipers loophole observed at G 6 a 65.85 about 10 yds to left of M.G. emplacement being shelled. At 8.30 am enemy aeroplane flew over 105 trench but on being shelled returned. Three squadrons of our aeroplanes came over from direction of DUISANS. About 15 enemy machines came over & engaged ours. One of our planes dropped a white light & a squadron retired. Ten minutes later another white light was dropped & all except 3 of our machines retired. They engaged enemy planes, & soon afterwards all retired. None was damaged. A Bosch was seen at G 6 a 7.2 wearing a steel helmet similar to ours. About 12 yards of our line was blown in in Trench 110 by T.M's & a dud 4.5 fell just outside Centre Coy H.Q. Work was continued as usual. AST. AST	
do	24.11.16		Our Stokes fired over 200 rounds in retaliation to enemy T.M's & rifle grenades. Our artillery dropped several shells short one falling in trench 106 & put a Lewis Gun out of action. Enemy T.M's fairly active all along our front. Generally each T.M was preceded by a rifle grenade. Our snipers shot a German, who had a badge like a grenade on his cap. In the morning several parties of the enemy were seen to come from B 14 a .2 .8 haystack & walk across the open for about 500 yds, & then go over the skyline. Work done by our troops revetting, clearing trenches blown in, & widening & deepening trenches AST	

Army Form C. 2118.

Instructions regarding War Diaries and Intelligence Summaries are contained in F. S. Regs., Part II. and the Staff Manual respectively. Title Pages will be prepared in manuscript.

WAR DIARY
or
INTELLIGENCE SUMMARY
(Erase heading not required.)

Place	Date	Hour	Summary of Events and Information	Remarks and references to Appendices
K1.	25.11.16		Two brilliant parachute lights were noticed on our right about 11.15 pm ~~A mine was exploded~~ Tapping was heard about 3.30 pm under shelter in sap leading to Kick Crater. Our Stokes were fairly active & mediums fired in co-operation with artillery	
do	26.11.16		A mine was exploded on our right at 2.25 am & S.O.S signal was sent up by Bn. on our right. A red green & a red light was sent up from Bn on our left at 2.59 am ~~At 11.5~~ Code word for gas discharge on our Div. front received at 11.5 pm the previous night & this was cancelled at midnight. It was received again at 1.15 am. At 2.40 am message was received from Bn on our right that Huns were in KING Crater. A company of Bn in Bde Res came up to Trench 50. ~~[illegible]~~ A.S.T. A little later news was received that King Crater was clear of the enemy & that the Bn on our left had re-occupied it. Situation normal was reported at 4 A.M. ~~[illegible]~~ Artillery & T.M's (enemy) comparatively quiet during the day. A few whiz bangs landed near Sunday Av. A number of enemy aeroplanes flew over our lines. A number of men were seen digging about G 6. b 9.3. A.S.T.	
do	27.11.16		~~Wiring party~~ Patrol reported that hostile wire was weak in front of Kent Crater. There was evidence of a good deal of ~~[illegible]~~ work in Hun line. ~~[illegible]~~ Considerable artillery activity was noticed well away to our left & a mine was heard to explode. Our troops carried on with usual work in trenches – revetting, cleaning, etc.	
do & Bde Res	28.11.16		Bn relieved by 17th Royal Scots. Bn went into Bde Res – one Coy at Rocklincourt, one in G. H. 9. & 2 works, one in E & F works & Thelus Redoubt & Observatory Fort, & one billeted in St Nicholas. H.Q. as previously at ARRAS. Coy at St Nicholas had 8 men per Coy attached to them for bombing class. A pioneer platoon (10 men from each Coy) under 2Lt Marshall started work under instructions from Bde. A.S.T.	

2449 Wt. W14957/M90 750,000 1/16 J.B.C. & A. Forms/C.2118/12.

Instructions regarding War Diaries and Intelligence Summaries are contained in F. S. Regs., Part II. and the Staff Manual respectively. Title Pages will be prepared in manuscript.

WAR DIARY
or
INTELLIGENCE SUMMARY
(Erase heading not required.)

Army Form C. 2118.

Place	Date	Hour	Summary of Events and Information	Remarks and references to Appendices
Bde Res	29-11-16		arrangements made for the men to have baths at Roclincourt. Some of W. Coy men bathed. W. Coy (in St Nicholas) supplied working party for ~~the~~ left Bn (K2) companies in posts etc. and much work, repairing trenches, wiring etc. AST	
do	30-11-16		Work continued in posts etc. W Coy again supplied working parties for left Bn. AST. Medical officer's report for week ending ~~[illegible]~~ 30/11/16 I inspected latrines in the line & found them all in good condition. New latrine was made in Falkland St. All the cookhouses were in good condition. An inspection of the stretcher bearers whilst rubbing the men's feet was satisfactory. The dugouts were kept clean & tidy H.W. Heasman M.O. 1/c 17th West Yorks. AST	

Instructions regarding War Diaries and Intelligence Summaries are contained in F. S. Regs., Part II. and the Staff Manual respectively. Title Pages will be prepared in manuscript.

WAR DIARY
or
INTELLIGENCE SUMMARY
(Erase heading not required.)

Army Form C. 2118.

17 W York Reg1
Vol XI

Place	Date	Hour	Summary of Events and Information	Remarks and references to Appendices
Bde Res & ARRAS	1.12.16		Received information at 8.30 AM that the Bde were to be relieved on 2nd inst. Orders were issued to Coys to be ready for relief. Officers of 6th K.O.S.B. came up to inspect the trenches. During the afternoon Bde issued orders that we were to ~~stay~~ stop in ARRAS, the men to be used as working parties. ast.	
ARRAS	2.12.16		Relieved in line by 6th K.O.S.B. Relief complete at 4 pm. Bn marched to billets, H.Q. being at 27 Rue des Capucines. Orders issued that we should find following working parties:- 110 men 6 AM, 110 men 2 pm, 130 men 10 pm all parties to report to New Zealand Tunnelling Coy ARRAS Station. ~~[illegible]~~ Parties were out between 9 & 10 hours. Bde H.Q. moved to FOUFFLIN RICAMETZ ast.	
do	3.12.16		Working parties the same as those of yesterday. C.O inspected billets ast	
do	4.12.16		Bn. continued to supply working parties. Weather dull & cold ast	
do	5.12.16		Working parties as usual. Arranged Baths for men at Rue de LILLE baths. ast	
do	6.12.16		Working parties as usual. Baths postponed as geyser was out of order. ast	
do	7.12.16		Working parties as usual Medical officer's report for week ending 7/12/16. All the billets clean. Accommodation for Coy officers ~~is~~ very limited. No latrine or washing accommodation for men when billets were taken over except in W & X Coys. This matter was taken in hand at once H.W. Heasman M.O. 1/c 17 W Yorks ast.	

2449 Wt. W14957/M90 750,000 1/16 J.B.C. & A. Forms/C.2118/12.

Instructions regarding War Diaries and Intelligence Summaries are contained in F. S. Regs., Part II. and the Staff Manual respectively. Title Pages will be prepared in manuscript.

WAR DIARY
or
INTELLIGENCE SUMMARY

(Erase heading not required.)

Army Form C. 2118.

Place	Date	Hour	Summary of Events and Information	Remarks and references to Appendices
ARRAS	8.12.16		Working parties as usual. Weather wet & cold AST	
"	9.12.16		Baths in Rue de Lille. No clean underclothing. Baths now taken over by 9th Div. Working parties as usual. AST.	
"	10.12.16		Working parties as usual. AST	
"	11.12.16		Working parties as usual. AST	
"	12.12.16		Working parties as usual. AST	
"	13.12.16		Received notice that ADMS wd inspect Bn on 14/12/16 with a view to weeding out unfit men. Letter from Div. stating that in re-organising Bn. C.O. must disregard "Bantam" standard & that standard of efficiency must be that of other Divisions of the Army. Working parties as usual. AST	
	14.12.16		Inspection by A.D.M.S. in X Coy billet. One hundred & fifty three (153) men marked D.P. etc. Working parties cancelled. AST.	
	~~15.12.16~~		~~Working parties as usual. Rest~~ [illegible] AST.	
			Medical officer's report for week ending 14/12/16. Latrine accomodation improved considerably, also washing accomodation. New billets in satisfactory condition. H.N. Heasman. M.O. i/c 17/West Yorks. AST.	
	15.12.16		Working parties as usual. Lists compiled by OC Coys of men whom they considered unfit to perform duties of a normal soldier. AST	
	16.12.16		Working parties as usual AST.	
	17.12.16		Working parties as usual. AST	
	18.12.16		Received orders to parade ~~men~~ men previously seen by A.D.M.S., also men selected by Coy Commanders for inspection by the Corps. Commander on 19/12/16. Remainder of Bn to be ready for inspection also. AST	
	19.12.16		Corps Commander inspected men. In addition to previous number marked by A.D.M.S., he picked out 115 as unsuitable. Working party in morning cancelled. AST.	
	20.12.16		Further lists of unfit men compiled by Coy Commanders. Total now reached 401. AST	

2449 Wt. W14957/M90 750,000 1/16 J.B.C. & A. Forms/C.2118/12.

Instructions regarding War Diaries and Intelligence Summaries are contained in F. S. Regs., Part II. and the Staff Manual respectively. Title pages will be prepared in manuscript.

WAR DIARY
or
INTELLIGENCE SUMMARY.

(Erase heading not required.)

Army Form C. 2118.

Place	Date	Hour	Summary of Events and Information	Remarks and references to Appendices
ARRAS	21.12.16		Working parties as usual. A.S.T.	
do	22.12.16		Working parties as usual. A.S.T.	
do	23.12.16		A.D.M.S visited Bn to inspect men of recent drafts of reinforcements marked "Unfit". A.S.T. M.O.'s report for week ending 21/12/16 Further latrine accomodation provided for officers & men X & Y Coy ~~moved to fresh~~ (A.S.T.) officers moved to new, & much better billets, also Z Coy officers. H.W. Heasman M.O. i/c 17th West Yorks A.S.T.	
do	24.12.16		Working parties as usual A.S.T.	
do	25.12.16		Working parties as usual with the exception of afternoon party for 184th Tun. Coy. Beer provided for men for Christmas Day. A.S.T.	
do	26.12.16		Received orders to parade all men recently picked out as unfit by Corps Commander & Coy Commanders as unfit at Dunsans at 11.30 A.M. 27/12/16 for inspection by the Army Commander Working parties as usual, with exception of 10 pm party A.S.T.	
do	27.12.16		Inspection, specified against date 26/12/16 took place. Working party at 6 A.M. had to be cut down on account of this. About 11 pm gas was detected in Streets of ARRAS. Weather calm & misty. Gas became thicker & helmets were put on. Coys stood to at their billets. Informed by 26 Bde that ~~shells~~ Huns were dropping gas shells in the town. Sentries reported hearing these shells. Gas cleared considerably by midnight ~~[illegible]~~ A.S.T.	
do	28/12/16		At 2.15 A.M. Strombos Horns were blown in the town & gas was again detected about billets. It soon cleared however & there was no further trouble. ~~A.S.T.~~ Received orders to move back to TERNAS on night of 29–30th	

A5834 Wt. W4973/M687 750,000 8/16 D. D. & L. Ltd. Forms/C.2118/13.

Instructions regarding War Diaries and Intelligence Summaries are contained in F. S. Regs., Part II. and the Staff Manual respectively. Title pages will be prepared in manuscript.

WAR DIARY
or
INTELLIGENCE SUMMARY.
(Erase heading not required.)

Army Form C. 2118.

Place	Date	Hour	Summary of Events and Information	Remarks and references to Appendices
ARRAS	29/12/16 ~~2/1/17~~		We furnished a working party of 120 men at 6 am only. 2nd Lt J. Marshall + 198 o.r. were left in ARRAS to furnish working parties for tunnelling coys. They were men considered unfit by Corps Commander + D.C Corps –	
			Batt. paraded at 5 p.m. and boarded Motor Lorries 6.30 p.m after being relieved by the 17th R.SCOTS. who had previously arrived in the aforesaid lorries. We proceeded to TERNAS, via DAINVILLE, WARLUS – WANQUENTIN, – AVESNES-LE-COMTE. It was a very wet night	
	30/12/16		TERNAS was reached at 2 a.m. and battalion settled in billets by 3 a.m.	
			Day spent in cleaning up. Weather still wet.	
			Billets were good so far as the officers were concerned; the mens billets were fair.	
			A draft of 177 R SCOTS. were left behind by their Bn. and were billetted in the village pending their despatch to Depôt Bn. 35th Div.	
	30/12/16		The Bn. sent all available officers & men to be fitted with the new small box-respirator at FOUFFLIN-RICAMETZ and the officers & men wore the helmets in tear gas to test them. No training was done. Day spent cleaning up.	
	31/12/16.		The following officers proceeded on a course at 3rd Army Inf. School at AUXI-LE-CHATEAU: Capt Mason, Capt Bell and Lieut Jenkins. A draft of ten men rejoined the Bn. this day.	
			Church Parade Service (C of E) was held	

A5834 Wt. W4973/M687 750,000 8/16 D. D. & L. Ltd. Forms/C.2118/13.

APPENDIX TO WAR DIARY

Appendix 1. 2Lt. G.E. Haddon to Hospl. Sick.
4.12.17

Appendix 2. Lieut. E.A. Parke joined from Base
4.12.17

Appendix 3 Draft of 56 O.R. joined from Base
4.12.17

Appendix 4 Lt. Col. W.B. Greenwell resumed
5.12.17 command

Appendix 5 Major V.E. Gooderson D.S.O.
6.12.17 rejoined 18th H.L.I.

Appendix 6 2Lieuts. C. Mosley, J. Murray
6.12.17 E.E. Lee, W.E. Lennard
joined from Base.

Appendix 7 Draft of 97 O.R. joined from Base
11.12.17

Appendix 8 2Lieuts. B. Donaldson & T. Hughff
12.12.17 joined from Base.

Appendix 9 2Lieut. R. Smith to Hospl Sick
15.12.17

Appendix 10 2Lieut. G.W. Johnson to England
19.12.17 – transfer to M.G.C.

Appendix 11 Lieut. J. Sharp joined from
21.12.17 Labour Corps.

Appendix 12 Lieut. Mc W.B. Jopling M.C. joined
23.12.17 from Base

Appendix 13 2Lt. H.V. Tyler to Hospl. Sick
26.12.17

appendix 14 | Lieut J. H. L. Nash - to Hospl. Sick.
29.12.17
appendix 15 | 30 Other Ranks, casuals, rejoined during the month.

Instructions regarding War Diaries and Intelligence Summaries are contained in F. S. Regs., Part II. and the Staff Manual respectively. Title pages will be prepared in manuscript.

WAR DIARY
or
INTELLIGENCE SUMMARY.
(Erase heading not required.)

Army Form C. 2118.

17. W York R

17 W York Regt

Vol 12

Place	Date	Hour	Summary of Events and Information	Remarks and references to Appendices
TERNAS	1/1/17		Day spent training men in Lewis Guns, Signalling and bombing. Working parties were sent to ST. FLOCHEL and also to work under R.E. in TERNAS at billet improvements	
	2/1/17		Training as usual also working parties as usual. A party of twenty men marked unfit proceeded to ARRAS to furnish working parties.	
	3/1/17		Training as usual. Working parties furnished to R.E. in TERNAS	
	4/1/17		All available men went to baths in four separate parties. Training went on as usual. A party of 3 men were sent to the base (unfit).	
	5/1/17		Training as usual	
	6/1/17		Training as usual. Six N.C.O.s were sent to Divisional Musketry School for training as instructors	
	7/1/17		Church Parade (C of E) was held at 12 noon. 2nd Lt Addington proceeded on a course to Divisional Infantry School.	
	8/1/17		Training as usual. All ranks armed with revolvers carried out revolver practise at the range. Lt Col Atkinson proceeded to a C.O's conference at AUXI-LE-CHATEAU and Maj. J. H. Gill took over command of the Battalion.	
	9/1/17		Training as usual. 2nd Lieut Battishill proceeded to ARRAS to take over the detachment there vice 2nd Lieut Marshall who proceeded to WIMEREUX to be attached to R.E.	
	10/1/17		All available men went to MAIZIERES. Training proceeded as usual. Draft of 67 men arrived. Sent direct to depot Bn for training	
	11/1/17		Training proceeded as usual	
	12/1/17		Training as usual. A further draft of 11 men was sent to join the detachment at ARRAS.	

Instructions regarding War Diaries and Intelligence Summaries are contained in F. S. Regs., Part II. and the Staff Manual respectively. Title pages will be prepared in manuscript.

WAR DIARY
or
INTELLIGENCE SUMMARY.
(Erase heading not required.)

17. W. York R

Army Form C. 2118.

Place	Date	Hour	Summary of Events and Information	Remarks and references to Appendices
TERNAS	13/1/17		Training proceeded as usual. Weather conditions very cold and wet. J.W.	
"	14/1/17		Church service (C of E) was held in the morning in the school room (TERNAS) ast	
			M.O.'s report for week ending 14/1/17. Inspection of underclothing revealed that they were free from scabies & fairly free from lice. This is attributed to regular bathing & regular clean issue of underclothing. H.W. [illegible] Capt RAMC MO 1/c 17 W. Yorks ast	
"	15/1/17.		Extremely cold weather. Great difficulty in keeping the men warm on parade. Training continued as usual. ast.	
"	16/1/17.		Draft of 29 men arrived. All with the exception of one man untrained. Two men sent to Hospital with Chr. Bronchitis. Another man sent away with measles. Remainder of men in billet isolated. ast	
"	17/1/17		Training as usual. Weather still very cold. ast	
"	18/1/17		do do do ast.	
"	19/1/17			
"	20/1/17			
"	21/1/17		Draft of 112 men arrived at 3 A.M. Of these 33 were trained 77 partially trained & the remainder untrained. A draft of 35 men arrived later in the day. Seven trained men amongst these ast	
	ast.		M.O.'s report for week ending 21/1/17. Cookhouses, with one exception, not very clean, & were short of various utensils. Some of those in possession not very clean. H.W. [illegible] Capt RAMC MO 1/c 17 W. Yorks ast	
"	22/1/17		Sniping & bombing & bayonet fighting classes arranged at Bde H.Q., FOUFFLIN RICAMETZ, also school for N.C.O.s & signallers Training at TERNAS as usual ast	
"	23/1/17		Continued training ast	
"	24/1/17		do ast	

A5834 Wt. W4973/M687 750,000 8/16 D. D. & L. Ltd. Forms/C.2118/13.

Instructions regarding War Diaries and Intelligence Summaries are contained in F. S. Regs., Part II. and the Staff Manual respectively. Title pages will be prepared in manuscript.

WAR DIARY
or
INTELLIGENCE SUMMARY.
(Erase heading not required.)

Army Form C. 2118.

Place	Date	Hour	Summary of Events and Information	Remarks and references to Appendices
TERNAS	25/1/17		Received notice of arrival of draft of 225 men ast	
"	26/1/17		Draft of 226 men arrived. Great majority of these men untrained. Usual training continued ast.	
"	27/1/17		Training as usual. Weather still very cold. ast.	
"	28/1/17		Received notice that Major A.R.H Drew 5th Bn. Northamptonshire Regt had been posted to this Bn.	
"	~~29/1/17~~		~~Training as usual~~. ast	
"	~~30/1/17~~		~~Received orders that the 35th Div. [illegible]~~ ast M.O.'s report for week ending 28/1/17: New draft men have been inspected by me as to their fitness. Any unfit have been brought to notice of A.D.M.S 35th Div. & any rejected by him have left Bn. H.W. Heasman Lt RAMS. M.O. 17th W. Yorks. ast	
"	29/1/17		Training as usual ast	
"	30/1/17		Received orders that the 35th Div. will march to BOUQUEMAISON area to join IV Corps on Feb 6th. Working parties in forward area to rejoin Bn. Orders also received to dig trenches in BEAUFORT training area ast	
"	31/1/17		Party of 100 ~~men went to ground near~~ DENIER to dig trenches for training. Training carried on as usual at TERNAS. Information received that men in ARRAS will rejoin Bn. on Feb 3rd. ast.	

A5834 Wt. W4973/M687 750,000 8/16 D. D. & L. Ltd. Forms/C.2118/13.

Instructions regarding War Diaries and Intelligence Summaries are contained in F. S. Regs., Part II. and the Staff Manual respectively. Title pages will be prepared in manuscript.

WAR DIARY
or
INTELLIGENCE SUMMARY.
(Erase heading not required.)

17 W York Regt

Vol 13

Army Form C. 2118.

Place	Date	Hour	Summary of Events and Information	Remarks and references to Appendices
Ternas	1/2/17		Sent 100 men to dig trenches near ~~Den~~ ast DENIER. These men attached temporarily to 17th R Scots at GOUY-EN-TERNOIS. Further 100 men sent to GOUY later in the day.	
"	2/2/17		Training as usual. Eight men marked Unfit by ADMS sent to Base, also two men for ~~[illegible]~~ (ast) Rab. Corps. ast.	
"	3/2/17		Training as usual. Weather remained very cold. ast	
"	4/2/17		Received intimation that 35th Div. will move from VI Corps area into BOUQUEMAISON area on Feb 6th. The Bn. was detailed to proceed to FORTEL on Feb 6th. ~~ast~~ ast.	
"	ast ~~5/2~~ ~~XX~~		Men who had been left behind as working party in ARRAS marched to TERNAS. One hundred & fifty two of these were detailed for the Base as unsuitable for offensive work. ast	
"	5/2/17		Men for Base, mentioned above, left TERNAS & entrained at AUBIGNY under two officers. Preparations made for tomorrow's move. ast Draft of 19 O.R. arrived. ast	
TERNAS & FORTEL	6/2/17		Bn. left TERNAS at 10.30 Am & arrived FORTEL, 3 pm. Six men who were unable to complete the march were brought along in the Ambulance ast	
FORTEL & OUTREBOIS	7/2/17		Left FORTEL at 10.15 & arrived at OUTREBOIS at 2 pm. Eight men were brought along in the Ambulance, owing mainly to sore feet. ast.	
~~[illegible]~~ & ~~[illegible]~~ ast			M.O's report for week ending 4/2/17. The incidence of sickness amongst officers & men during the week has been quite low. The men have had baths week by week, & I attribute the low sickness rate amongst the men to the good personal hygiene & good and sufficient food. H. W. Heaseman Lt. RAMC. M.O. i/c 17 W. Yorks. ast.	

A5834 Wt. W4973/M687 750,000 8/16 D. D. & L. Ltd. Forms/C.2118/13.

Instructions regarding War Diaries and Intelligence Summaries are contained in F. S. Regs., Part II. and the Staff Manual respectively. Title pages will be prepared in manuscript.

WAR DIARY
or
INTELLIGENCE SUMMARY.
(Erase heading not required.)

Army Form C. 2118.

Place	Date	Hour	Summary of Events and Information	Remarks and references to Appendices
OUTEBOIS to HAVERNAS	8.2.17		Left OUTREBOIS for HAVERNAS at 9.45 Am, arriving HAVERNAS 6.30 pm. AST	
HAVERNAS	9.2.17		Company commanders selected training grounds, a musketry range, & bombing ground were also found. Programmes of work made out. Eleven O.R. sent to Bn. as re-inforcements. All Signallers. AST	
"	10.2.17		Major P.S. Hall rejoined the Bn. and took over the duties of 2nd in Command. AST Training re-commenced. Instruction in musketry, bombing, etc under specialist officers. Physical training, bayonet-fighting & drill etc formed part of the days work. Weather still very cold. AST	
"	11.2.17		Parade services:- R.C's 9. Am, C of E 3.30 P.M. Inspection of new draft men who arrived Feb 5 & 9 by C.O & M.O. All were passed "Fit". AST	
"	12.2.17		Training continued. Inspection of Transport at VIGNACOURT. Concert for the men 5 pm to 7 p.m. AST	
"	13.2.17		Training continued. Scheme of wiring carried out by all Companies. Commenced bathing the men under regimental arrangements. Clean clothing for 220 men only available. Concert for the men in the evening AST.	
"	14.2.17		Training as usual. Bathing continued. AST	
"			M.O's report for week ending 14/2/17. Only a few men were evacuated during march from TERNAS to HAVERNAS. Extra latrine accomodation at HAVERNAS has brought the number of seats up to 41. On account of having to move again materials are not available for completing the number of seats up to 52. Av. Health good. RAMC M.O. 7th N. W. [illegible]. AST	
"	15.2.17		Training & bathing. Received orders to move to area South of the SOMME. Transport to start on 18.2.17, & Bn. to entrain at VIGNACOURT on 19.2.17 AST	
"	16.2.17		Training carried on as usual. AST.	
"	17.2.17		do do AST	

A5834 Wt. W4973/M687 750,000 8/16 D. D. & L. Ltd. Forms/C.2118/13.

Army Form C. 2118.

Instructions regarding War Diaries and Intelligence Summaries are contained in F. S. Regs., Part II. and the Staff Manual respectively. Title pages will be prepared in manuscript.

WAR DIARY
or
INTELLIGENCE SUMMARY.

(Erase heading not required.)

Place	Date	Hour	Summary of Events and Information	Remarks and references to Appendices
HAVERNAS	18·2·17		Preparations made for move on 19th inst. Transport left for MARCELCAVE by road. AST. Major P. S. Hall left Bn to take command of 15th Cheshire Regt AST	
HAVERNAS & MARCELCAVE	19·2·17		Bn. left HAVERNAS at 10 am & marched to VIGNACOURT to entrain. Train left station at 12 noon. Arrived MARCELCAVE station 2·45 pm. In billets 3·10 pm AST	
MARCELCAVE	20·2·17		Training continued during the day. Good deal of the work had to be done under cover owing to bad weather AST	
do	21·2·17		Received orders to move to CAIX on 22/2/17. Training as usual. AST MO's report for week ending 21/2/17. Troops on the march & very few fell out. Health of the men remains good. There have been very few men sick lately. H W Heasman Lt RAMC, MO 7/c 17th W Yorks. AST	
MARCELCAVE & CAIX	22·2·17		Left MARCELCAVE at 12·17 pm, ARRIVED CAIX 2·30 pm. Roads in a very bad condition which made marching very difficult. Transport proceeded to Camp des BALLONS. AST	
CAIX	23·2·17		Training carried on during the day. Conditions very bad AST Lt Col. H.R.H. Drew admitted to Hospital. Major Gill took over command of the Bn. AST	
CAIX & Camp des BALLONS	24·2·17		Left CAIX at 9·30 AM for Camp des BALLONS. AST which was reached at 10·30 AM. FRENCH huts in the wood fairly good. Wood in a very bad state. Thick mud all over. Training carried on during the afternoon. AST	
CAMP DES BALLONS	25·2·17		Training carried on. Received orders to take over trenches in LIHONS sector. AST	

A5834 Wt. W4973/M687 750,000 8/16 D. D. & L. Ltd. Forms/C.2118/13.

Instructions regarding War Diaries and Intelligence Summaries are contained in F. S. Regs., Part II. and the Staff Manual respectively. Title pages will be prepared in manuscript.

WAR DIARY
or
INTELLIGENCE SUMMARY.
(Erase heading not required.)

Army Form C. 2118.

Place	Date	Hour	Summary of Events and Information	Remarks and references to Appendices
CAMP des BALLONS & Trenches (LIHONS SECTOR)	26.2.17		Left Camp des BALLONS at 11 A.M. & marched to ROSIERES. Halted here until dusk. Moved up to the trenches in LIHONS sector at 5.30 pm AST Front held — A 4 c 2.0 (left) to A 15 a 75.50 right. Bn H.Q. A 8 d 7.4 Reference sheet 66(e) N.E., 66(d) N.W. (parts of) AST	
Trenches	27.2.17		Our artillery shelled roads behind enemy lines during the early morning. Retaliation slight. Work done in clearing communicating trenches. One O.R. killed (accidentally). AST	
"	28.2.17		No retaliation to our bombardment of enemy's line south of DEMI LUNE. At mid-day a white very light which burst into numerous stars was sent up opposite DEMI LUNE, & several salvoes of Whizz-bangs resulted. During our shelling in the evening, enemy sent up several red lights which broke into three red stars. E of BOIS BROWNIG enemy has cut some of our wire & laid a tape to this point. Work:- clearing & draining of trenches; latrines made AST	

17th West Yorks. Regt. 106/35 Army Form C. 2118.

Vol 14

Instructions regarding War Diaries and Intelligence Summaries are contained in F. S. Regs., Part II. and the Staff Manual respectively. Title pages will be prepared in manuscript.

WAR DIARY
or
INTELLIGENCE SUMMARY.
(Erase heading not required.)

Place	Date	Hour	Summary of Events and Information	Remarks and references to Appendices
Trenches LIHONS Sector	1.3.17		Enemy was fairly quiet, except for snipers. About mid-day a white Very light sent up opposite the DEMI LUNE burst into numerous stars & was followed by several salvoes of Whiz-bangs. In the evening our artillery bombarded trenches in front of centre Coy. There was no retaliation. AST	
"	2.3.17		Artillery (enemy) shelled continuously from 10.30 am to 5 pm. especial attention being paid to the right Coy. A T.M. emplacement was located opposite the DEMI LUNE. Our troops did much work cleaning trenches etc. AST.	
" " " "	3.3.17 4.3.17 5.3.17 6.3.17		Bn. occupied support trenches. Working parties were supplied daily for work on the trenches etc. Attack on the DEMI LUNE was expected on the night of 4.3.17 & Bn stood to. The attack was not made. AST	
"	7.3.17		Bn occupied front line trenches, relieving 19th D.L.I. Our artillery cut wire on North side of the DEMI LUNE. Enemy artillery was active & T.M's were directed on the DEMI LUNE during the afternoon AST	
"			M.O's report for week ending 7.3.17. The trenches were extremely muddy & it was very difficult to make drying arrangements for socks, but the mens feet were rubbed twice daily with whale oil. In spite of this some cases of oedema of the feet occurred. Latrines were erected as far as possible H. W. Heasman M.O. i/c 17th W. Yorks. AST	
"	8.3.17		Enemy artillery very active on DEMI LUNE. Intense bombardment during early evening. Raiding party of about 20 men entered our trenches. Casualties were 1 killed 1 wounded & 5 missing (believed taken prisoners) AST	

Instructions regarding War Diaries and Intelligence Summaries are contained in F. S. Regs., Part II. and the Staff Manual respectively. Title pages will be prepared in manuscript.

WAR DIARY
or
INTELLIGENCE SUMMARY.
(Erase heading not required.)

17th. West Yorks Regt. Army Form C. 2118.

Place	Date	Hour	Summary of Events and Information	Remarks and references to Appendices
LIHONS SECTOR	9.3.17		Enemy's T.M's very active on our left during the morning. Our artillery shelled enemy's lines North of Railway. There was very little sniping during the day. ast	
	10.3.17.		Our artillery shelled intermittently during the day. There was not much retaliation. 18. H.L.I. relieved the Bn. at night. Bn moved to billets in ROSIERES. Owing to bad condition of trenches three platoons of the right Coy could not be relieved. Owing to a change of the Bn. fronts this Coy was to have been relieved by the 17th R. Scots. ast	

A5834 Wt. W4973/M687 750,000 8/16 D. D. & L. Ltd. Forms/C.2118/13.

Instructions regarding War Diaries and Intelligence Summaries are contained in F. S. Regs., Part II. and the Staff Manual respectively. Title pages will be prepared in manuscript.

WAR DIARY
or
INTELLIGENCE SUMMARY.
(Erase heading not required.)

17th. West Yorks Regt.

Army Form C. 2118.

Place	Date	Hour	Summary of Events and Information	Remarks and references to Appendices
ROSIERES	11.3.17		Men rested & commenced cleaning up ~~AST~~ RT. Coy's relief completed AST	
do	12.3.17		Working parties supplied. Classes for Bombers & Lewis Gunners held. Baths at 107th Field Ambulance. AST	
do	13.3.17		Working parties etc. same as on 12.3.17. AST	
ROSIERES & DECAUVILLE CAMP	14.3.17		Bn. moved to DECAUVILLE CAMP. Arrived in camp 5 pm. AST	
DECAUVILLE CAMP	15.3.17		Preparations made for practising the assault. Orders received at 10 pm that the Bn would relieve 23rd Manchester Regt (104th Bde) in CHILLY sector on night of 16.3.17. AST	
do & CHILLY SECTOR	16.3.17		Bn sent up advance parties to CHILLY SECTOR to take over stores etc. Bn left DECAUVILLE CAMP at 2.30 pm. Conveyed in motor lorries to VRELY where guides were met. Bn. came under orders of G.O.C. 104th Bde. Took over trenches from 23 Manchester Regt AST	
CHILLY Sector	17.3.17		At 2.30 p.m. Bn entered GERMAN front line which had been evacuated. An officer went to FRANSART & ~~[illegible]~~ (AST) here also there were none of the enemy. Orders received that the Bn were to move tomorrow to MENELAS trench & ~~[illegible]~~ (AST) occupy the line between G 2.c 6.9.8 G 2.b 0.2 (Sheet 66E.NE & 66 d N.W (parts of) AST.	
do	18.3.17		Bn. pushed on ~~[illegible]~~ further & reached HATTENCOURT. There were no signs of the enemy. The railway line was demolished. Village heavily mined. AST	

A5834 Wt. W4973/M687 750,000 8/16 D. D. & L. Ltd. Forms/C.2118/13.

Instructions regarding War Diaries and Intelligence Summaries are contained in F. S. Regs., Part II. and the Staff Manual respectively. Title pages will be prepared in manuscript.

WAR DIARY
or
INTELLIGENCE SUMMARY.

(Erase heading not required.)

Army Form C. 2118.

17th West Yorks Regt.

Place	Date	Hour	Summary of Events and Information	Remarks and references to Appendices
HALLU	19·3·17		Bn. moved to HALLU & bivouacked. Reconnaisance of country to the East was made. AST.	
do	20·3·17.		Working parties supplied for mending roads. Two companies reported at MAUCOURT at 6 AM & two at 6 pm. AST	
do	21·3·17		Working parties again supplied. Two Coys reported 12 noon instead of 6 pm. Brig. Gen. Commanding 104th Infy Bde & Brig. Gen. Commanding 106th Infy Bde congratulated Bn on the work done on 17th & 18th inst. They especially congratulated 2Lt Rose, Lt Jenkins & 2Lt White for their patrolling work. AST.	
			M.O.'s report for week ending 21·3·17. The Bn was in the trenches which were three or four feet deep in mud. Under these trying conditions some men became affected with swollen feet but not more than cd be expected. H.W. Hearnman M.O. 17th West Yorks. Rgt. AST.	
do	22·3·17		Working parties again supplied. Lewis Gun class held by 2Lt Thurgood (6 men per Coy) Bombing class also held by 2nd Lt de W-Lt (15 men per Coy) AST	
do	23·3·17.			
do	24·3·17.		Working parties & training. In 106th Infy Bde orders dated 23/3/17. G.O.C. congratulated Lieut Col. H.R.H. Drew, Officers, Non-commissioned officers & men of the Bn. on being the first Bn of the Div. to enter the enemy lines at the commencement of the present advance on March 17th. He also specially congratulated Lt H.F.O. Jenkins & 2Lt A.D. Rose on the excellent work performed by the patrols under their command. AST	

Instructions regarding War Diaries and Intelligence Summaries are contained in F. S. Regs., Part II. and the Staff Manual respectively. Title pages will be prepared in manuscript.

WAR DIARY
or
INTELLIGENCE SUMMARY.
(Erase heading not required.)

Army Form C. 2118.

17th West Yorks Regt.

Place	Date	Hour	Summary of Events and Information	Remarks and references to Appendices
HALLU	25.3.17		Working parties continued. One officer & 4 N.C.O's sent for instruction under Div. Bombing officer in the use of the rifle grenade. AST	
do	26.3.17		Working parties. Bn. Bombing officer held class of instruction in the use of the rifle grenade. AST	
do	27.3.17		Orders received that the 106 Infy Bde would move to new area immediately East of the SOMME on 29.3.17, with Bde H.Q probably at MARCHELEPOT, & the Bns. in the villages in the vicinity. Working parties continued. AST	
do.	28.3.17		Baths provided for the Bn. at 107th Field Amb. ROSIERES Working parties cancelled. Orders received that Bn. will move to POTTE tomorrow. AST.	
HALLU ~~POTTE~~	28.3.17		M.O's Report for week ending 28/3/17. Bn has for the last week been in bivouack. All the men had a bath & clean change of underclothing. Health of the men remains good. H. W. Heasman M.O. i/c 17th W. Yorks Regt. AST	
HALLU POTTE	29.3.17		Bn moved to POTTE arriving there 1 pm. Weather very wet & stormy. Officers & men billeted in cellars, dug-outs & barns. Most of the buildings had been rendered uninhabitable. Working parties ordered to be provided for tomorrow AST	
POTTE	30.3.17		Working parties provided for road mending etc. Classes of instruction carried on by specialist officers, also company training for offensive. AST	
do	31.3.17		Working parties & training as usual. AST	

A5834 Wt. W4973/M687 750,000 8/16 D. D. & L. Ltd. Forms/C.2118/13.

Instructions regarding War Diaries and Intelligence Summaries are contained in F. S. Regs., Part II. and the Staff Manual respectively. Title pages will be prepared in manuscript.

17th West Yorks Regt

WAR DIARY
or
INTELLIGENCE SUMMARY.

(Erase heading not required.)

Army Form C. 2118.

Vol 15

Place	Date	Hour	Summary of Events and Information	Remarks and references to Appendices
POTTE	1.4.17		Working parties as usual & training under specialists. AST	
do	2.4.17		do do do do do AST	
POTTE PARGNY & FALVY	3.4.17		Bn moved to PARGNY & FALVY, two Coys & H.Q. to PARGNY & two Coys to FALVY. Bn, less men detailed for training under specialist officers, engaged in repairing & draining road from PARGNY to ENNEMAIN. AST	
PARGNY & FALVY	4.4.17		do do do do AST	
do & ENNEMAIN	5.4.17		Working parties & training as usual. Bn moved to ENNEMAIN. AST	
ENNEMAIN	6.4.17		Working parties knocked off at noon. Bn practiced the attack during the afternoon & evening AST	
do	7.4.17		Work on the road extended to MONTECOURT. Training under specialists continued. AST	
~~do~~ AST	~~8.4.17~~		MO's report for week ending 7/4/17. Health of men was good on the whole. A bath house was fixed up & men were bathed. G.W. Heasman Lt RAMC M.O. 17th W. Yorks AST	
do	8.4.17		Working parties the same as usual. Training under specialist officers continued AST.	
MONCHY LAGACHE & TERTRY	9.4.17		Bn moved to MONCHY LAGACHE (three Coys) & TERTRY (Bn H.Q. & one Coy) AST	
~~do~~ VERMAND	10.4.17		Bn moved to VERMAND. Working parties supplied for work on roads AST	

A5834 Wt. W4973/M687 750,000 8/16 D. D. & L. Ltd. Forms/C.2118/13.

Instructions regarding War Diaries and Intelligence Summaries are contained in F. S. Regs., Part II. and the Staff Manual respectively. Title pages will be prepared in manuscript.

17th West Yorkshire R. 17th

WAR DIARY
or
INTELLIGENCE SUMMARY.
(Erase heading not required.)

Army Form C. 2118.

Place	Date	Hour	Summary of Events and Information	Remarks and references to Appendices
VERMAND.	11·4·17		Three Coys required for filling craters & repairing roads. One Coy had the whole day for training. AST	
do	12·4·17		do do do do AST	
do	13·4·17		do do do do AST	
do	14·4·17		Working parties in the morning. During the afternoon preparations were made for moving into the line. Bn relieved 19th D.L.I. in the line in PONTRU area. Bn H.Q. at BIHECOURT. AST	
			M.O.'s report for week ending 14.4.17. There were number of cases [struck through] AST impetigo, otherwise there were very few sick. Water was obtained from the stream. A.W. Heasman Lt RAMS M.O. i/c 17th W. Yorks. AST	
Trenches PONTRU area	15·4·17		Our artillery very active at 4 am. After some considerable time enemy dropped 15 H.E. shells in the wood M 7.d (Sheet 62 B. S.W) No damage was done. Outpost positions were sighted & work on them was started AST	
	16·4·17		Trenches deepened & improved. Slit-trenches were also made. There was intermittent shelling during the day by the enemy who sent over a large number of "duds". On the night of 15th & early morning 16th one officer & 25 men patrolled the front. There was no trace of the enemy in portions of M.2.c & M 2 d (Sheet 62 B.S.W) through which he had passed while working last. At a point about [struck through] AST M 3.c.1.8 patrol discovered that the enemy were established about 20 yards away. They appeared to be about 15 strong & they opened fire on our patrol. Our officer was wounded & ordered patrol to retire, as enemy position was too strong to be taken from that flank. AST	

A5834 Wt. W4973/M687 750,000 8/16 D. D. & L. Ltd. Forms/C.2118/13.

Instructions regarding War Diaries and Intelligence Summaries are contained in F. S. Regs., Part II. and the Staff Manual respectively. Title pages will be prepared in manuscript.

WAR DIARY
or
~~INTELLIGENCE SUMMARY.~~
(*Erase heading not required.*)

17th West Yorkshire Regt

Army Form C. 2118.

Place	Date	Hour	Summary of Events and Information	Remarks and references to Appendices
Trenches PONTRU area	17.4.17		Raid was made on German front line trenches on ridge North of PONTRU between M.3 d 3.8 & M 3 b 2.2 (Sheet 62B. S.W. 1/20,000). Strength of raiding party 3 officers & 100 men; covering party 2 officers & 40 men. Covering party first encountered enemy's advanced sentries who retired to a crater M 3. 0.7. Crater was rushed, & enemy retired so quickly that no prisoners were taken. At 11.50 pm (16/4/17) raiding party passed through covering party & advanced under our artillery barrage. The wire in front of German trenches was very strong & devoid of gaps. Enemy opened M.G. fire on our men. Two platoons however pressed on & cutting gaps in the wire rushed through & entered enemy trenches which were strongly occupied. On close approach of our men garrison left the trenches & ran. Rapid fire was opened on him & several casualties were inflicted. Our box barrage prevented our party from proceeding further to collect identifications from enemy's dead. Some rifles were brought back. Casualties 8 wounded 10 missing. AST	
do	18.4.17		It was noticed that enemy has been working on trenches behind BELLENGLISE. Our troops continued to improve trenches & ~~[illegible]~~ AST. strengthen the wire. Bn was relieved by 19th Durham Light Infantry. One Coy attached to this Bn. Other three Coys & Bn H.Q. proceeded to SOYECOURT. AST	
SOYECOURT	19.4.17		Working parties for repair of roads etc provided AST.	
do	20.4.17		do do do do do AST.	
do	21.4.17		Working parties. Baths provided for men at VERMAND. AST	
do	22.4.17		M.O.'s report for week ending 21/4/17 All the men were bathed. The health of the men remained good H.W. Heasman Lt RAMC M.O. i/c 17th W Yorks AST	

A5834 Wt. W4973/M687 750,000 8/16 D. D. & L. Ltd. Forms/C.2118/13.

Instructions regarding War Diaries and Intelligence Summaries are contained in F. S. Regs., Part II. and the Staff Manual respectively. Title pages will be prepared in manuscript.

WAR DIARY
or
~~INTELLIGENCE SUMMARY.~~

(Erase heading not required.)

17th West Yorkshire Regt.

Army Form C. 2118.

Place	Date	Hour	Summary of Events and Information	Remarks and references to Appendices
SOYECOURT	22.4.17		Working parties provided. Two companies worked on front-line trenches at night. ast.	
do	23.4.17		Working parties & training under specialist officers as usual. One Coy attached to 19th D.L.I. in the line returned to the Bn. Five shells were sent by enemy near Coys billeted in wood ~~...~~ east of SOYECOURT no damage done. ast	
do	24.4.17		Companies employed road mending. ast	
do	25.4.17		Working parties & training under specialist officers as usual. Baths were provided by 105th Field Amb. at VERMAND. Very little clean clothing was provided. ast.	
do	26.4.17			
do	27.4.17		Bn. practised the attack. The G.O.C Division (Major General H. D. S Landon C.B) presented Military Medal to No 1616 a/C.S.M Ryle, No41543 Pte Walsh, No41611 Pte Mitelow, & No641 Pte Bridgement. Medals were awarded for gallant conduct during the raid on German trenches, referred to in this diary against date 17.4.17. ast	
do	28.4.17		Working parties provided for road mending etc. Every available man employed. Specialist classes cancelled. ast	
do	29.4.17		Coys practised the attack, ~~...~~ ast. patrols, etc. Orders received that Bn would relieve 14th Gloucester Rgt in the line at FRESNOY & GRICOURT. ~~On~~ the night of 30 ap/1 May. ast	
do	30.4.17		Bn relieved 14 Gloucester Rgt in the line at FRESNOY & GRICOURT. ast.	

H. N. Stew[?] Lt Col
Cmdg 17th W. Yorks. Rgt.

A5834 Wt. W4973/M687 750,000 8/16 D. D. & L. Ltd. Forms/C.2118/13.

Army Form C. 2118.

Instructions regarding War Diaries and Intelligence Summaries are contained in F. S. Regs., Part II. and the Staff Manual respectively. Title pages will be prepared in manuscript.

WAR DIARY
or
INTELLIGENCE SUMMARY.
(Erase heading not required.)

Vol 16

Place	Date	Hour	Summary of Events and Information	Remarks and references to Appendices
LINE FRESNOY-GRICOURT area	1.5.	17	Enemy shelled ridge at M27 d (Sheet 62 b S W) also FRESNOY & GRICOURT. AST.	
	2.5.	17	Enemy artillery active all day. Considerable activity in the air on both sides. Our trenches improved. Patrol of 1 officer & 23 O.R. found LES TROIS SAUVAGES unoccupied. On reaching point M24 a 3.6 (Sheet 62 b S.W.) enemy opened fire on our scouts, two of whom were hit. They were taken back to aid post. Patrol heard enemy working near LE CATELET - ST QUENTIN Rd. AST.	
do	3.5.	17	Enemy shelled LES TROIS SAUVAGES with heavies & L.H.V. Patrol of 2 officers & 31 other ranks reconnoitred new enemy trenches east of Les TROIS SAUVAGES. On approaching LES TROIS SAUVAGES farm, our scouts were fired on from the farm & from position half left. Our Lewis gunners & rifle bombers opened fire & did good work, enemy fire eventually dying down. Patrol advanced, firing from the hip but were held up by concertina wire. Enemy re-opened fire, but our men scrambled through the wire & gained the road in front of the farm. We took one prisoner (a/pte 234th 11 Coy, 453rd I.R. ERS. Res.) The farm was searched & found to be clear. Another officer & 20 men sent out as support- then came up & were sent forward on the left of the farm. Temporary posts were established on each flank of the farm, which was thoroughly patrolled. A few shots were fired from a point about 70 yds to the right. We replied & three Germans ran away across the open. As orders had been issued not to keep posts on the flank of the farm during daylight the whole party returned without casualties. Erection of new wire indicated that enemy intended to occupy the farm. Object of patrol not attained because there was not time, the opposition met with at the farm accounting for this. AST.	
do	4.5.	17	Work was begun on new posts adjacent to LES TROIS SAUVAGES. Enemy opened intense bombardment & firing was good. As there was insufficient cover & casualties were increasing, the position became untenable & party was withdrawn. Bn was relieved by 19th Durham Light Infantry. AST.	

A5834 Wt. W4973/M687 750,000 8/16 D. D. & L. Ltd. Forms/C.2118/13.

Army Form C. 2118.

Instructions regarding War Diaries and Intelligence Summaries are contained in F. S. Regs., Part II. and the Staff Manual respectively. Title pages will be prepared in manuscript.

WAR DIARY
or
INTELLIGENCE SUMMARY.
(Erase heading not required.)

Place	Date	Hour	Summary of Events and Information	Remarks and references to Appendices
Reserve Trenches FRESNOY GRICOURT & ~~Holnon~~ ST QUENTIN WOOD ast	5·5·17		Bn. H.Q. & one Company bivouacked in St QUENTIN WOOD; three Companies occupied reserve line. Two of our Coys relieved two Companies of the 19th D.L.I. to enable them to carry out operations. They were relieved in the early hours of the morning & took up their former positions. ast	
do	6·5·17		Work was continued on the line near FRESNOY, were being strengthened & fire steps etc. made. German aeroplane was brought down on our right. ast	
do	7·5·17		Work carried on as yesterday. Artillery shelled LES TROIS SAUVAGES from 11.5 pm to 11.50 pm. ast	
do	8·5·17		Bn. relieved by 14th Glosters, & returned to former bivouacks at SOYECOURT. ast	
SOYECOURT	9·5·17 10·5·17 11·5·17		Working parties & training. Baths provided at VERMAND. ast	
do	12·5·17		100 men went to musketry school at PONT REMY. Two officers & 100 men attached to 105th Bde for work. ast	
	13·5·17		Working parties provided to fill crater at BEUILLY. ast	
	14·5·17		Training under Coy arrangements in accordance with Bde instructions, & also under specialist officers. ast MO's Report for week ending 14·5·17. Apart from boils health of the men good. Latrine accommodation improved. J A C Greene MO 1/c 17th W Yorks ast	

A5834 Wt. W4973/M687 750,000 8/16 D. D. & L. Ltd. Forms/C.2118/13.

Instructions regarding War Diaries and Intelligence Summaries are contained in F. S. Regs., Part II. and the Staff Manual respectively. Title pages will be prepared in manuscript.

WAR DIARY
or
INTELLIGENCE SUMMARY.
(Erase heading not required.)

Army Form C. 2118.

Place	Date	Hour	Summary of Events and Information	Remarks and references to Appendices
Soyecourt	15.5.17		Bn engaged in working parties. AST	
do	16.5.17		Training. AST.	
do	17.5.17		Training etc. AST	
do	18.5.17			
PERONNE	19.5.17		Moved to billets in PERONNE. AST.	
do	20.5.17		One Coy sent to new camping area near SOREL LE GRAND to pitch tents for Bn. & for Bde H.Q. AST.	
SOREL LE GRAND	21.5.17		Moved to camp near SOREL LE GRAND. Coy Commanders went into new line for the night. AST.	
do	21.5.17		MO's report for week ending 21.5.17. Number of minor ailments but health of the men, on the whole, good. Water supply in camp at SORREL LE GRAND plentiful. J.A.C. Greene MO i/c 17th W. Yorks. AST	
Trenches	22.5.17		Training near camp. AST.	
	23.5.17		Relieved 20th Middlesex Regt in trenches east of VILLERS GUISLAIN, with Bn H.Q at that place. Patrols reported wire weak along our front. Parties sent out to begin strengthening the wire	
Trenches	24.5.17		Patrol of 1 off. & 15 men went out to see if enemy occupied posts at X5d 2.9 (Sheet 57c SE) No trace of enemy was found. Another patrol of three Officers & 22 O.R. reconnoitred ground near X5b 6.3 (Sheet 57c SE) Enemy observed near entrance to STICK-RAVINE but retired immediately on patrol advancing. Men seen walking about from HONNECOURT along main road to RANCOURT FARM. VILLERS GUISLAN was shelled during the day. Work – wiring, draining & improving trenches. AST	

A5834 Wt. W4973/M687 750,000 8/16 D. D. & L. Ltd. Forms/C.2118/13.

Instructions regarding War Diaries and Intelligence Summaries are contained in F. S. Regs., Part II. and the Staff Manual respectively. Title pages will be prepared in manuscript.

WAR DIARY
or
INTELLIGENCE SUMMARY.
(*Erase heading not required.*)

Army Form C. 2118.

Place	Date	Hour	Summary of Events and Information	Remarks and references to Appendices
Trenches	25.5.17		Slight enemy artillery activity. Aeroplanes fired M.G's into our front line. Our artillery shelled HONNECOURT & selected points. Aeroplanes active. One German machine brought down. Strong patrol proceeded along road to X 11 a 9.9. & on to house shown aerial photos. Enemy were present in ruins of house & opened fire on patrol. Another patrol of 3 officers & 25 O.R. reconnoitred TWENTY TWO RAVINE to R.36 a 5.0. (Sheet 57c S.E) They advanced down ravine for about 400 yds & patrol was divided into four sections. They advanced in this formation to their destination, the road junction, the better road running NORTH through a cutting in the left side of the ravine. Cutting was strongly wired. 2Lt Moore with the advance section passed through the obstruction & found himself face to face with 4 Germans. He fired & one man was heard to groan. Fire was returned & the enemy ran off, throwing two stick bombs, one of which wounded 2Lt Moore. Patrol proceeded along track which leads S.W. from R.36 a 5.0. & enemy fired on them but there were no further casualties. Work — wiring, improving trenches etc. AST	
do	26.5.17		Our artillery shelled LA TERRIERE & BANTOUZELLE. A few enemy gas shells fell around quarry R 34 a 8.8. Patrol went out to see if post on road X 5 Central (Sheet 57c SE) was held. Patrol was fired on but advanced & found post unoccupied, enemy having withdrawn. Work carried on as usual. AST	
do	27.5.17		About 4.15 pm enemy raided our No 2 post at X 5 c 5.1. Enemy, about 4 strong worked their way up the bank on the left side of the road. They fired on the sentry & then rushed forward keeping well under the bank. They then threw hand grenades & seriously wounded the sentry who was dragged out by the Germans & taken away. One of our men threw a bomb at the enemy but it failed to explode. The patrol made off down the road dragging the sentry with them. They were fired on but escaped. Three other men in the post were wounded. At night new posts were dug & ~~[illegible]~~ strongly wired. Patrol reconnoitred sunken road	

A5834 Wt. W4973/M687 750,000 8/16 D. D. & L. Ltd. Forms/C.2118/13.

Army Form C. 2118.

Instructions regarding War Diaries and Intelligence Summaries are contained in F. S. Regs., Part II. and the Staff Manual respectively. Title pages will be prepared in manuscript.

WAR DIARY
or
INTELLIGENCE SUMMARY.
(Erase heading not required.)

Place	Date	Hour	Summary of Events and Information	Remarks and references to Appendices
Trenches	27.5.17 (cont)		in front of left Coy front to ascertain if it would be suitable for front line. It was considered that a trench sited along the road would be under flank observation from the left rear, thus it was not thought to be suitable for occupation as a front line. Work as usual. a.s.t	
"	28.5.17.		At 7.30 am Sgt. Watson (No 16139) Left Coy went out along the side of the road which leads from the right of the left Coy through X 5 Central (Sheet 57c S.E.) He found enemy occupying a post near X 5 d 3.8. He fired at & wounded one of the enemy & afterwards hit another one in the stomach as he came forward to assist his comrade. Four more men then appeared & Sgt. Watson came back quietly. The post in question is 375 yds in front of the advanced post on the right of Left Coy front. At 7 pm enemy artillery from E of HONNECOURT registered on the left Coys trench between Post 6 & 10 with about 25 H.E. Shells. No casualties. An enemy working party was observed about 1800 yds away & was fired on by one of our L.G.s. Two men were hit. Bn was relieved by 19 Durham Light Infantry.	
"	28.5.17.		M.O's report for week ending 28.5.17. Whilst in the line very few men reported sick. Latrine accomodation was improved & water was taken up the line in Petrol tins from VILLERS GUISLAIN. J. A. Greene M.O. 1/c 17th West Yorks. a.s.t	
VILLERS GUISLAIN	29.5.17		Bn engaged at night carrying material to line; wiring, work on roads etc. VILLERS GUISLAIN heavily shelled during the morning. Capt. E.G. HADOW, M.C. killed by shell. a.s.t	
"	30.5.17		Work as on previous night. VILLERS again shelled during the day. a.s.t	

Army Form C. 2118.

WAR DIARY
or
INTELLIGENCE SUMMARY.
(Erase heading not required.)

Instructions regarding War Diaries and Intelligence Summaries are contained in F. S. Regs., Part II. and the Staff Manual respectively. Title pages will be prepared in manuscript.

17(S) Bn. West Yorks. Rgt.

Place	Date	Hour	Summary of Events and Information	Remarks and references to Appendices
VILLERS GHISLAIN	31.5.17		104th Bde took over 1 Coy front of 106th Bde, dividing line being X 5 a 55, track to X 4 c 3.3, road to X 3 c 60.15 to GENIN WELL COPSE No 2 (Sheet 57c S.E.) One Coy of this Bn. moved from billets in VILLERS to bivouacs in Railway embankment near VAUCELETTE FARM. A second Coy was accomodated in Green Line. Bn was engaged at night wiring right Bn front, improving trenches etc, & carrying material to the front line.	

[illegible] Lt. Col.
Comdg 17(S) Bn West Yorks. Rgt

A5834 Wt. W4973/M687 750,000 8/16 D. D. & L. Ltd. Forms/C.2118/13.

Instructions regarding War Diaries and Intelligence Summaries are contained in F. S. Regs., Part II. and the Staff Manual respectively. Title pages will be prepared in manuscript.

WAR DIARY
or
INTELLIGENCE SUMMARY.
(Erase heading not required.)

Army Form C. 2118.

VA 17

Place	Date	Hour	Summary of Events and Information	Remarks and references to Appendices
VILLERS GUISLAN	1.6.17		Bn in support. Enemy shelled village during the day. All available men employed at night in the line – wiring, digging, carrying etc. AST	
"	2.6.17		Bn relieved by 15 Sherwood Foresters (105th Infy. Bde). Two companies employed carrying R.E. material to the line before relief. Bn moved to camp at TEMPLEUX LA FOSSE. AST	
TEMPLEUX LA FOSSE	3.6.17		Day of rest. Baths provided for three Companies. AST.	
"	4.6.17		Inspections etc. Training in the evening AST	
"	5.6.17		Baths for remainder of Bn. Training, 8 hours. AST.	
"	6.6.17		Training carried on as usual. Lt Col. P.S. Hall. D.S.O. took over	
"	7.6.17		command of the Bn. 7/6/17. vice Lt Col. H R H Drew, posted to 5th Northants. Rgt. AST	
			M.O's report for week ending 7/6/17. Bath for the men made in the camp. Field oven constructed. Latrines improved. Health of the Bn good. G.A.C Green Lt RAMC M.O. i/c 17 W. Yorks. AST	
"	8.6.17		Training as usual. AST	
"	9.6.17			
LINE, VILLERS GUISLAIN Sector	10.6.17		Bn. took over the line from 20th Lancs. Fus. in VILLERS GUISLAIN sector. Patrols sent out at night reported everything quiet & no signs of the enemy up to 600x in front of our line. Work done. Improving trenches & wire. AST	

A5834 Wt. W4973/M687 750,000 8/16 D. D. & L. Ltd. Forms/C.2118/13.

Instructions regarding War Diaries and Intelligence Summaries are contained in F. S. Regs., Part II. and the Staff Manual respectively. Title pages will be prepared in manuscript.

WAR DIARY
or
INTELLIGENCE SUMMARY.
(Erase heading not required.)

Army Form C. 2118.

Place	Date	Hour	Summary of Events and Information	Remarks and references to Appendices
VILLERS GUISLAIN Sector	11.6	17	An O.P. was established in left post of support Coy X 4 a 4.6. (Sheet 57 C S.E) Patrol (1 off & 5 men) went out from our front line, & when about 50 yards in front of our second belt of wire, were bombed by a German patrol. Enemy made use of bank R.34 d 9.8 to R 35 c 5.6 (Sheet 57 C. SE) to approach our line. The officer in charge of patrol & three of the men were wounded, but in spite of this, rapid fire was opened on the Germans, who retreated hurriedly. A party that went out afterwards found five German stick bombs. Enemy shelled ground between our front & support lines during the afternoon. VILLERS GUISLAIN was shelled during the day. Snipers on ridge on left flank were active. Searchlight played in sky from the direction of HAVRINCOURT WOOD. Work done. Trenches improved, wire strengthened. AST	
"	12.6.17		Artillery fairly active all day. Two German aeroplanes flew low over VILLERS early in the morning. Listening patrol (1 off & 5 O.R) with a Lewis Gun established at R 35 c 3.7 (Sheet 57 C. SE) with the object of wiping out expected German patrol. Small listening post was pushed out, & they heard some one crawling towards them. They withdrew to the Lewis Gun position & warned the party. [illegible] AST. Nothing further was seen or heard of the enemy. AST	
"	13.6.17		Our artillery fairly active. Enemy little quieter than usual although VILLERS was shelled intermittently. Listening patrol was again sent out as on the night of 12/6/17, & a small German patrol was heard advancing. They were alarmed by a noise from our line, & went back. Five enemy planes over our line during the day were driven off by anti aircraft guns. AST	

A5834 Wt. W4973/M687 750,000 8/16 D. D. & L. Ltd. Forms/C.2118/13.

Instructions regarding War Diaries and Intelligence Summaries are contained in F. S. Regs., Part II. and the Staff Manual respectively. Title pages will be prepared in manuscript.

WAR DIARY
or
INTELLIGENCE SUMMARY.
(Erase heading not required.)

Army Form C. 2118.

Place	Date	Hour	Summary of Events and Information	Remarks and references to Appendices
VILLERS GUISLAIN sector	14.6.17		Hostile artillery shelled our front line at R34 d 8 4 (Sheet 57 C. S.E.) VILLERS was also shelled. During the afternoon two very fast machines flew over our lines. One was light blue colour with a white tail numbered 2. The other had grey fuselage, buff wings & a tail numbered either 5 or 6. They were driven off by our guns. Search light was again used. Bn was relieved by 19th Durham Light Infantry. ast	
	15		M.O's report for week ending 14/6/17. Latrines erected. Health of the men good. Number of sick while in the line very small. J.A.C. Greene Lt. RAMC M.O i/c 17th W. Yorks. ast	
Camp near HEUDICOURT	15.6.17		Working parties for R.E. Two Companies worked at night on the Green Line in front of GAUCHE WOOD. ast	
"	16.6.17		Work as on 15.6.17. ast	
"	17.6.17		Ditto. ast	
"	18.6.17		ditto. Corps Com. presented Military Medal to 161395 Sgt. I. Watson P.D. ast	
"	19.6.17		ditto ast	
"	20.6.17		ditto ast	
"	21.6.17		ditto ast	
"	21.6.17		M.O's report for week ending 21.6.17. Bath was made for the men in the Camp. Field ovens constructed. Health of the men good. Impetigo not so common. J.A.C. Greene Lt. RAMC M.O i/c 17th W Yorks ast	
" VILLERS GUISLAIN Sector	22.6.17		Bn relieved 19th Durham Light Infy, right Bn. VILLERS GUISLAIN sector. ast	

A5834 Wt. W4973/M687 750,000 8/16 D. D. & L. Ltd. Forms/C.2118/13.

Instructions regarding War Diaries and Intelligence Summaries are contained in F. S. Regs., Part II. and the Staff Manual respectively. Title pages will be prepared in manuscript.

WAR DIARY
or
INTELLIGENCE SUMMARY.
(Erase heading not required.)

Army Form C. 2118.

Place	Date	Hour	Summary of Events and Information	Remarks and references to Appendices
VILLERS GUISLAIN sector	23.6.17		~~Two strong listening patrols were sent out after relief of 19 D.L.I.~~ ast Two patrols reconnoitred positions for parties to act as covering parties to men digging new trenches on the night of the 23/24. Searchlight played on GONNELIEN at 9 on our line. Light came from direction of LATERRIERE. Our trenches were improved. ast	
"	24.6.17		Two strong listening patrols were sent out up the BANTEUX RAVINE to act as covering party to men digging new trenches in front of the left Bn. Patrol on the right was fired on by rifles & M.G's. From 7.30 am to 1.30 pm enemy shelled GAUCHE WOOD heavily. VILLERS GUISLAIN was also shelled. Our front line was shelled during the afternoon & one direct hit damaged seven rifles & some L.G magazines. No casualties. Movement was seen in BANTOUZELLE. M.G. fired from R29d 45.65 (57c S.E. 1/20,000) ast.	
"	25.6.17		Listening patrols again went out. About 11 pm two ~~of the enemy~~ men ast came across BANTEUX RAVINE towards the right covering party. They were challenged & at the same time three men got up in front of the covering party & ran for the German lines. They were fired on, but apparently got away. There was heavy bombardment on our right at night. Six large red flares as of from explosions were seen at 12.45 pm behind enemy lines in the direction of LESDIN. During an bombardment enemy sent up several successions of red lights on which their artillery fired. At 1.15 pm two enemy aeroplanes flew over our lines. One dived to within about 100 ft of the ground & fired his M.G. into our front line. We retaliated with rifles & Lewis Guns. ast	
"	26.6.17		Digging operations on our left continued up to daylight. One man of one of the covering parties was killed by shell fire. No signs of the enemy. There	

A5834 Wt. W4973/M687 750,000 8/16 D. D. & L. Ltd. Forms/C.2118/13.

Instructions regarding War Diaries and Intelligence Summaries are contained in F. S. Regs., Part II. and the Staff Manual respectively. Title pages will be prepared in manuscript.

WAR DIARY
or
INTELLIGENCE SUMMARY.
(Erase heading not required.)

17TH (S.) BATTALION, WEST YORKSHIRE REGT.
No. ....
Date ....

Army Form C. 2118.

Place	Date	Hour	Summary of Events and Information	Remarks and references to Appendices
VILLERS GUISLAIN Sector	26.6.17		(cont). There was desultory shelling of our front line during the day. Of 12 4.2's fired on the right Coy 8 were duds. GONNELIEU was shelled during the day, a number of heavies fell into VILLERS. Germans were seen walking about the buildings at R23. a. 8.5 (Sheet 57.C.S.E. (1/20,000)) During the morning enemy aeroplanes came over our line South of VILLERS but were driven back by anti-aircraft guns. Four machines patrolled our lines between 4 pm & 8 pm. Work in line was carried on as usual. Bn was relieved by 15th Cheshire Rgt. & proceeded to camp to AIZECOURT LE BAS. ast	
AIZECOURT LE BAS.	27.6.17.		Day spent in cleaning up, inspections etc. ast.	
"	28.6.17		Training. Musketry, Lewis Gun, Bombing, attack etc. Baths at TEMPLEUX LA FOSSE. ast M.O.'s report for week ending 28/6/17. Health of the men remained good. Construction of latrines in the line carried on. J.A.C. Campbell MO i/c 17th W. Yorks. ast.	
"	29.6.17		. Training as usual. ast	
"	30.6.17		Do. ast.	

P. J. Hall Lt Col
Comdg 17° West Yorks.

A5834 Wt. W4973/M687 750,000 8/16 D. D. & L. Ltd. Forms/C.2118/13.

7th (S) Bn. W. York R.

Instructions regarding War Diaries and Intelligence Summaries are contained in F. S. Regs., Part II. and the Staff Manual respectively. Title pages will be prepared in manuscript.

WAR DIARY
or
INTELLIGENCE SUMMARY.
(Erase heading not required.)

July 1917

Army Form C. 2118.

Vol 18

Place	Date	Hour	Summary of Events and Information	Remarks and references to Appendices
AIZECOURT LE BAS	1.7.17		Training. AST	
do 9 LIERAMONT	2.7.17		Bn moved to Lieramont. AST	
LIERAMONT	3.7.17		Bn. took part in a practise attack by 106th Infy. Bde. AST	
do	4.7.17		Training AST	
do	5.7.17		do AST	
do	6.7.17		Relieved the Carbineers (6th D.G.) in C. I Sub Sector. Relief complete 12.10 am 7th inst. AST	
C I Sub-sector	7.7.17		Enemy artillery fairly active on our left. Work in our line included improvement of trenches building latrines etc. AST M.O's report for week ending 7.7.17. Boils & Impetigo rather prevalent. Otherwise, health of the men good (Sd) J. Young Capt, RAMC. M.O. i/c 17th W. Yorks AST	
"	8.7.17		Road leading to advanced "A" post was shelled during the night but no damage was done. Digging was done by enemy on the ridge to the right of 11 trees. COLOGNE FARM trench mortared during the morning. The glow of a large fire was seen behind enemy lines. AST	
"	9.7.17		Germans were seen digging on the top of the ridge to the right of the 11 trees. Enemy heavily shelled C & B posts for about 15 minutes at night. Two casualties. This barrage was probably called for by a German who fired a white very light towards our own lines. Work done – finishing trench between B post & C1 post, also wiring. Generally improving line AST	
"	10.7.17		Hostile artillery fairly active during the day. A train was heard to arrive somewhere behind BONY at about midnight. In the evening E.A. dropped 1 white & shortly afterwards one green & one red light. Soon afterwards enemy commenced shelling	

A5834 Wt. W4973/M687 750,000 8/16 D. D. & L. Ltd. Forms/C.2118/13.

Army Form C. 2118.

WAR DIARY
or
INTELLIGENCE SUMMARY.
(Erase heading not required.)

Instructions regarding War Diaries and Intelligence Summaries are contained in F. S. Regs., Part II. and the Staff Manual respectively. Title pages will be prepared in manuscript.

Place	Date	Hour	Summary of Events and Information	Remarks and references to Appendices
C1 Sub sector	10.7.17		(cont) Our snipers hit a German 1500 yds away. A&T	
C1 Sub sector	11.7.17		A Post & Hussar Post shelled from 6.45 pm to 8.30. ~~Two~~ No casualties (Cadey). Little damage 50% duds. A few shells in front of Lone Post during the night. At 5 pm 3 shells behind ORCHARD POST. Usual amount of movement observed. E.A. over our lines 3.45 pm & 6 pm. Enemy plane observed shelling of A POST. Sounds of sapping reported in front of RIFLE PIT TRENCH. Work done on new trench between GILLEMONT FARM & C1 POST. Also improving own trenches. Our snipers claim one victim. Cadey	
— " —	12.7.17		Our Artillery fairly active in counter shelling. Enemy artillery active, especially between 8 & 9 a.m., & 4.30 & 5 p.m. "A" POST & HUSSAR POST again shelled the latter being damaged in 3 places. A large proportion of duds. At 12 midnight enemy opened heavy fire with guns & T.Ms in front of C1 POST. S.O.S. went up on our left & artillery fired on S.O.S. lines. All quiet by 1 a.m. No damage done to our trenches. Three casualties. Little movement seen during the day. E.A passed over our lines several times during the day & at 10.30 a.m. enemy plane flew very low over our front line. Work done on new trench & our own trenches. Cadey	
— " —	13.7.17		Enemy artillery again active, "A" & HUSSAR POSTS receiving most of the attention. 2nd Lt SOWRY buried during shelling of "A" POST & slightly bruised. Forty enemy seen haymaking ~~and~~ (Cadey) & 15 men entered BONY. E.A fairly active at 8 p.m. a patrol of 6 E.A. came over our lines & was driven off by A.A & Lewis gun fire. Work done on new trench & our own lines. Cadey	
— " —	14.7.17		At 2 a.m. heavy shelling opened on our front & that of battalion on our right, whence the S.O.S was sent up. Artillery opened on S.O.S. lines. Enemy raided battalion on our right. We had no casualties. Few minutes before the bombardment started a red light was flashed from high ground in enemy's lines. This is thought to be a signal to recall patrols & forward Very light men. At 7 p.m. our artillery carried out a shoot on enemy's front line & (Cadey) QUENNET COPSE. Enemy retaliated with ~~[illegible]~~ (Cadey) 4.2's & 5.9's all along our front. 3 killed, 2 wounded in B. POST. Between 7 & 8.15 a.m. enemy shelled 'A' & 'B' Posts with 5.9s. Three killed & three wounded in B POST. 10.30 to 11.30 a.m. enemy shelled C POST with 77 m & H.E. shrapnel. No damage. 2 Enemy planes were observing during 7 to 8.15 a.m. shelling. They were fired on by A.A. At 12 midnight 200 gas shells were fired into BONY. ~~[illegible]~~ (Cadey) Cadey	

Instructions regarding War Diaries and Intelligence Summaries are contained in F. S. Regs., Part II. and the Staff Manual respectively. Title pages will be prepared in manuscript.

WAR DIARY
or
INTELLIGENCE SUMMARY.
(Erase heading not required.)

Army Form C. 2118.

Place	Date	Hour	Summary of Events and Information	Remarks and references to Appendices
C1 Sub Sector	14/7/17	(contd.)	M.O.'s report for week ending 14/7/17 — Boils less prevalent owing to extra ration of Lime Juice & to the fact that vegetables & fruit have been obtainable. Otherwise, health good. (Sd) J. A. C. Greene. Lt R.A.M.C. i/c 17th West Yorks Regt. Cadell	
— " —	15/7/17		Enemy Artillery quieter. Between 9 a.m. & 10 a.m. about 40. 4.2's were fired on the right of our front, gradually traversing to in front of HUSSAR POST. No damage. About 40% duds. 11 a.m. about 15 L.H.V. into saps on right of C POST. A POST lightly shelled with 4.2's about 5.30 p.m. Lt Cohen slightly wounded in head & left hand. 9.30 p.m. enemy fired about 10 rounds 4.2 into Quarries at TEMPLEUX-LE-GERARD. Battalion was relieved by 19th D.L.I. & proceeded to billets in Quarries at TEMPLEUX-LE-GERARD. Relief complete 11.40 p.m. The enemy had 5 balloons up between 7.30 and 8.45 p.m. This delayed relief. Cadell	
Quarries TEMPLEUX LE GUERARD	16/7/17		Baths during the day. Working party on new line between CAT POST & GILLEMONT FARM at night. Work done on Hardy Road during the day. Cadell	
— " —	17/7/17			
	18/7/17			
	19/7/17			
	20/7/17		Between 5 p.m. & 8 p.m. about 500 × 4.2's (H.E. & shrapnel) fell between Hardy Road & the Quarries. No damage done. Work at Hardy Bank & duckboarding new trench during the day & usual work on new line at night. Cadell	
	21/7/17		Between 8 a.m. & 2 p.m. about 1200 shells fell between Hardy Road & the Quarries, mostly 4.2 H.E. 4 Shelters blown in in Hardy Road. One man of W Coy wounded. Duckboarding new trench by day continued. Usual work on new line at night. Also 30 men working in Rifle Pit trench. Cadell. M.O.'s report for week ending 21/7/17 – Health of the men good. (Sd) J. A. C. Greene Lt R.A.M.C. i/c 17th West Yorks Regt. Cadell	

A5834 Wt. W4973/M687 750,000 8/16 D. D. & L. Ltd. Forms/C.2118/13.

Army Form C. 2118.

Instructions regarding War Diaries and Intelligence Summaries are contained in F. S. Regs., Part II. and the Staff Manual respectively. Title pages will be prepared in manuscript.

WAR DIARY
or
INTELLIGENCE SUMMARY.
(Erase heading not required.)

17TH (S.) BATTALION, WEST YORKSHIRE REGT.

Place	Date	Hour	Summary of Events and Information	Remarks and references to Appendices
Quarries TEMPLEUX LE GUERARD	22/7/17		Work done on Hardy ~~Road~~ ROAD Cadell & duckboarding new trench by day. Usual work on new trench at night. Work on RIFLE PIT TRENCH was stopped at 1.15 a.m. by persistent Rifle Grenade Fire. Cadell	
—"—	23/7/17		Work finished on Hardy Road & duckboarding new trench by day-light continued. The Battalion was relieved by 16th Battn. Cheshire Regt. without incident & marched to camp at ~~Day~~ Cadell AIZECOURT-LE-BAS. Relief complete 11.35 p.m. Cadell	
AIZECOURT LE BAS	24/7/17		Day spent in cleaning up & inspections Cadell.	
—"—	25/7/17		Bayonet Fighting for whole battalion on Brigade Assault Course Cadell.	
"	26.7.17		Training ast	
"	27.7.17		Training ast	
"	28.7.17		Training, including Bde Inter-platoon shooting Competition ast MO's report for week ending 28/7/17. Health of the men remains good. J.A.C. Greene Lt, R.A.M.C. MO i/c 17th W Yorks ast	
"	29.7.17		Training. ast	
"	30.7.17		Training in the morning. Bde Sports in the afternoon. ast	
"	31.7.17		Left AIZECOURT to relieve ~~Relieved~~ ~~2nd~~ Glosters in C.I Sub Sector (LEMPIRE). ~~ast~~ Arrived at VILLERS FAUCON & were informed that relief was postponed. Returned to AIZECOURT. ast	

R P Hall Lt Col
Comdg 17th West Yorks

A5834 Wt. W4973/M687 750,000 8/16 D. D. & L. Ltd. Forms/C.2118/13.

Army Form C. 2118.

17 W York Rgt

Vol 19

Instructions regarding War Diaries and Intelligence Summaries are contained in F. S. Regs., Part II. and the Staff Manual respectively. Title pages will be prepared in manuscript.

WAR DIARY
or
INTELLIGENCE SUMMARY.
(Erase heading not required.)

Place	Date	Hour	Summary of Events and Information	Remarks and references to Appendices
AIZECOURTLE BAS. & EPEHY sector.	1.8.17		Relieved 18 Lancs. Fus. in EPEHY sector. Relief complete 11.10 pm. AST	
EPEHY sector	2.8.17		Very quiet all day. Weather extremely bad. Commenced improving the trenches, & wire. Rum issued to the men. AST	
"	3.8.17		again very quiet. Wiring round Birdcage improved AST	
"	4.8.17		Two Germans seen outside dugout at X23 d 9.4 (Map Δ Corps Topo Sec 7) disappeared when fired on. Work of improving trenches proceeded with. Patrol reported enemy in FALCON SAP. AST	
LEMPIRE & RONSSOY	5.8.17		Stokes guns fired on FALCON SAP. Artillery co-operated. Very little retaliation. Bn. relieved by 19. Durham Light Infy. proceeded to billets in LEMPIRE AST	
"	6.8.17		Received news of raid on GILLEMONT FARM. Bn. stood-to at 4.15 am "Situation normal" received 4.40. am. Working parties supplied during the day & at night. AST	
LEMPIRE & RONSSOY & LINE	7.8.17		Received orders to take over Centre Bn. front from 18th H.L.I. Relief complete 10.45 pm. AST M.O's report for week ending 7/8/17. Health of the men good. Number of sick fairly small. Latrine accommodation improved (Sd). Jac Greene, Lt. RAMC M.O. i/c. 17th W. Yorks. AST	
LINE	8.8.17.		Very quiet during the day & night. AST	
"	9.8.17		New assembly trench shelled by the enemy during the day. AST	
"	10.8.17		En. Artillery registered on F. post. En. wiring party at the KNOLL fired on & were dispersed. Wire at the KNOLL	

A5834 Wt. W4973/M687 750,000 8/16 D. D. & L. Ltd. Forms/C.2118/13.

Instructions regarding War Diaries and Intelligence Summaries are contained in F. S. Regs., Part II. and the Staff Manual respectively. Title pages will be prepared in manuscript.

WAR DIARY
or
INTELLIGENCE SUMMARY.
(Erase heading not required.)

Army Form C. 2118.

Place	Date	Hour	Summary of Events and Information	Remarks and references to Appendices
LINE	10.8.17		(cont) patrolled & found to be strong. Relieved by 16 Cheshires & 17. Royal Scots. AST.	
RONSSOY	11.8.17		} Supplied working parties for digging cable trenches, constructing dug-outs etc. AST	
"	12.8.17		}	
"	13.8.17		}	
RONSSOY & LINE	14.8.17		Relieved 17th Royal Scots & 18 H.L.I. in GILLEMONT FARM, CAT POST, DOLEFUL POST. Relief complete 12 midnight. AST M.O's report for week ending 14/8/17. Health of men much as usual. Number of minor ailments. Lt-Col. Greene M.O. 17th W Yorks AST	
LINE	15.8.17		Good deal of movement behind German lines. Very quiet at night. AST	
"	16.8.17		Our artillery registered on GILLEMONT FARM. Considerable amount of work done improving trenches at the FARM. AST.	
"	17.8.17 ~~[illegible]~~		Orders received for 35 Div. attack on GILLEMONT FARM & the KNOLL. Bn. relieved in GILLEMONT FARM, D post & D1 Post by 18 Highland Light Infy. CAT POST still held by us. ~~AST~~ Three Coys billeted in RONSSOY, Bn HQ in LEMPIRE AST	
LEMPIRE RONSSOY, & the line	18.8.17		Working party supplied for RE. 4 men killed near D1 post. AST	
	19.8.17		GILLEMONT FARM & the KNOLL attacked by Bns. on our left. Trenches taken & consolidated. Counter attack by the enemy in the evening repulsed. CAT POST shelled during the day. Some casualties inflicted. AST	
	20.8.17		Working parties for RE & M.G. Coy supplied. BASSE BOULOGNE North & South & LEMPIRE West posts taken over by the Bn. AST.	

Instructions regarding War Diaries and Intelligence Summaries are contained in F. S. Regs., Part II. and the Staff Manual respectively. Title pages will be prepared in manuscript.

WAR DIARY
or
INTELLIGENCE SUMMARY.

(Erase heading not required.)

17TH (S.) BATTALION, WEST YORKSHIRE REGT.
No.
Date

Army Form C. 2118.

Place	Date	Hour	Summary of Events and Information	Remarks and references to Appendices
LEMPIRE RONSSOY & LINE	21.8.17		Battery positions in RONSSOY heavily shelled by enemy. AST M.O.'s report for week ending 21/8/17. Health of men good. J.A.C. Greene Lt. RAMS. M.O. 1/c 17 W. Yorks	AST.
"	22.8.17		Working parties for R.E. supplied. AST	
"	23.8.17		do do AST	
"	24.8.17		Bn relieved by 17th D.L.I. Proceeded to camp at VILLERS FAUCON. AST	
VILLERS FAUCON & ST EMILIE	25.8.17.		Bn ordered to proceed to ST EMILIE to support counter attack on GILLEMONT FARM which enemy re-captured in the morning AST	
ST EMILIE	26.8.17		Wiring party (130 O.R.) supplied for R.E. AST	
The KNOLL	27.8.17.		Bn relieved 16th Cheshires & part of 14th Glosters in the KNOLL & adjacent posts. AST	
"	28.8.17.		Enemy quiet. Bn did much work cleaning up trenches. AST	
"	29.8.17.		Good deal of movement seen behind enemy lines. KNOLL shelled intermittently during the day AST.	
"	30.8.17		KNOLL shelled & trench mortared throughout the day AST	
"	31.8.17		Enemy attacked & re-captured the KNOLL at 4.45 am after intense artillery & Trench Mortar bombardment. Our casualties were:- Officers 2 killed 5 missing 6 wounded (3 at duty) O.R. 7 killed, 56 wounded 53 missing Bn relieved by 17 R Scots & proceeded to VILLERS FAUCON. AST	

A5834 Wt. W4973/M687 750,000 8/16 D. D. & L. Ltd. Forms/C.2118/13.

R J [illegible] Lt Col
Comdg 17th W. Yorks

Instructions regarding War Diaries and Intelligence Summaries are contained in F. S. Regs., Part II. and the Staff Manual respectively. Title pages will be prepared in manuscript.

WAR DIARY
or
INTELLIGENCE SUMMARY.
(*Erase heading not required.*)

Army Form C. 2118.

Vol 2

Place	Date	Hour	Summary of Events and Information	Remarks and references to Appendices
VILLERS FAUCON + AIZECOURT-LE-BAS	1.9.17		Battalion relieved in the KNOLL by 17th Royal Scots + went into camp at VILLERS FAUCON. Left camp at 5pm. + went into camp at AIZECOURT-LE-BAS. M.O.'s report for week ending 1/9/17. Health of men fairly good. Prevailing sickness Impetigo. Sd J.A.C. Greene. Lieut. R.A.M.C. i/c 17th West York Regt. Cadell	
AIZECOURT-LE-BAS	2.9.17		Refitting & Inspections. Cadell.	
—"—	3.9.17		Training. Battalion inspected by G.O.C. 106th Infy Bde. Cadell.	
—"—	4.9.17		—"— —"— G.O.C. 35th Division. Cadell.	
—"—	5.9.17		Training. Cadell.	
—"—	6.9.17		Training during the morning. Battalion relieved part of 23rd Manchester Regt + part of 17th Lancs. Fus. Regt in Brigade Support in EPEHY Sector. Cadell	
Bde Support. E of EPEHY.	7.9.17		Working parties (wiring & digging) supplied for the BIRDCAGE. ast	
			M.O.'s report for week ending 7.9.17. Health of the men good. Lt. J.A.C. Greene M.C. RAMC. 17th W. Yorks. ast	
do	8.9.17 9.9.17 10.9.17 11.9.17		Working parties supplied for digging trench at the BIRDCAGE. Small parties found for RE'S. ast	
Front Line (BIRDCAGE)	12.9.17		Relieved 19th D.L.I. in the Birdcage, HEYTHROP Post + CRUCIFORM Post. ast	

A5834 Wt. W4973/M687 750,000 8/16 D. D. & L. Ltd. Forms/C.2118/13.

Instructions regarding War Diaries and Intelligence Summaries are contained in F. S. Regs., Part II. and the Staff Manual respectively. Title pages will be prepared in manuscript.

WAR DIARY
or
INTELLIGENCE SUMMARY.
(Erase heading not required.)

Army Form C. 2118.

Place	Date	Hour	Summary of Events and Information	Remarks and references to Appendices
BIRDCAGE Sector	13.9.17		Intermittent shelling during the day. ast	
do	14.9.17		Enemy heavily bombarded our line at 12.10 am. Rapid rifle & machine gun fire was at once opened by our troops, & our artillery was immediately called upon. Daylight patrol discovered some stick & egg bombs near the S. end of OSSUS Wood. There were no signs of dead Germans or of equipment. ast our casualties. Wounded 1 officer & 11 O.R. Killed 4 O.R. M.O's report for week ending 14.9.17. Apart from one or two cases of impetigo & P.U.O. health of the men normal. (sd) Lt. J.A.C. Greene M.C. RAM.C. 17th W. Yorks. ast	
do	15.9.17		Very quiet both day & night.	
do	16.9.17		Raid by Bn. on our left. BIRDCAGE shelled & trench mortared soon after our bombardment began. Casualties 3 O.R killed 6 O.R wounded.	
do	17.9.17		Intermittent shelling. Our troops wired & repaired damage done by shell fire. ast	
do & VILLERS FAUCON	18.9.17		Bn relieved by 15 Sherwood Foresters. ~~ast~~ Bn marched to billets in VILLERS FAUCON. ast	
VILLERS FAUCON	19.9.17		Cleaning up etc. ast	
"	20.9.17		Training, baths, & working parties. ast	
"	21.9.17		do ast	

A5834 Wt. W4973/M687 750,000 8/16 D. D. & L. Ltd. Forms/C.2118/13.

Instructions regarding War Diaries and Intelligence Summaries are contained in F. S. Regs., Part II. and the Staff Manual respectively. Title pages will be prepared in manuscript.

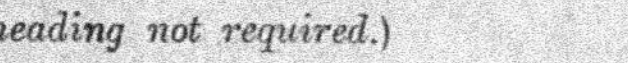

WAR DIARY
or
INTELLIGENCE SUMMARY.
(Erase heading not required.)

Army Form C. 2118.

Place	Date	Hour	Summary of Events and Information	Remarks and references to Appendices
VILLERS FAUCON	21.9.17		M.O's report for week ending 21.9.17. Health of men satisfactory (Sd) Lt J. A. C. Greene M.C. RAM.C. AST	
do	22.9.17 23.9.17 24.9.17 25.9.17		Training as usual. Working parties continued AST	
LEMPIRE.	26.9.17		Relieved 18 Lancs. Fus. in LEMPIRE. AST.	
do	27.9.17.		Working parties etc. AST	
do	28.9.17		do AST	
			M.O's report for week ending 28.9.17. Health of the men continues satisfactory. (Sd) Lt J. A. C Greene M.C. RAM.C. AST	
LEMPIRE & FLEECEALL & GRAFTON POSTS.	29.9.17		Relieved 19 D.L.I. in FLEECEALL & GRAFTON POSTS & SART LANE. Relief completed without incident. AST	
do.	30.9.17		Desultory shelling by the enemy during the day. Night patrols handicapped by brilliant moonlight. AST.	

[illegible] Lt Col
Cmdg 17 (S) Bn W. Yorks. Rgt.

A5834 Wt. W4973/M687 750,000 8/16 D. D. & L. Ltd. Forms/C.2118/13.

Instructions regarding War Diaries and Intelligence Summaries are contained in F. S. Regs., Part II. and the Staff Manual respectively. Title pages will be prepared in manuscript.

WAR DIARY
or
~~INTELLIGENCE SUMMARY.~~
(Erase heading not required.)

17TH (S.) BATTALION, WEST YORKSHIRE REGT.
No. .... Date October 1917

Vol 27

Army Form C. 2118.

Place	Date	Hour	Summary of Events and Information	Remarks and references to Appendices
FLEECEALL & E G O Posts	1.10.17		Battery positions in LEMPIRE heavily shelled during the day. AST	
Bn H. Q. LEMPIRE	2.10.17		Bn relieved by 1/6th Kings Liverpool Rgt. ~~ast~~ Bn marched to VILLERS FAUCON AST	
VILLERS FAUCON	3.10.17		Bn moved to PERONNE en route for ARRAS. AST	
AGNEZ LES DUISANS	4.10.17		Bn moved by train to ARRAS, & marched to camp at AGNEZ LES DUISANS AST	
do	5.10.17		Inspections etc. AST	
do	6.10.17		Training. AST	
do	7.10.17		Training. AST MO's report for week ending 7.10.17. Apart from a few cases of boils health of men good (S) J A.C. Greene M.C. R.A.M.C. M.O. 17 W. Yorks. AST	
do	8.10.17		Training AST	
do	9.10.17		do AST	
do	10.10.17		do AST	
do	11.10.17		do AST	
do	12.10.17		do AST	
do	13.10.17		Left AGNEZ LES DUISANS for ARRAS en route to RUDBROOK AST.	
RUDBROOK	14.10.17		Bn in RUDBROOK. AST M.O.'s report for week ending 14.10.17. Health of the men good. AST Lt J A C. Greene M.C. RAMC. M.O. 17 W Yorks	

A5834 Wt. W4973/M687 750,000 8/16 D. D. & L. Ltd. Forms/C.2118/13.

Instructions regarding War Diaries and Intelligence Summaries are contained in F. S. Regs., Part II. and the Staff Manual respectively. Title pages will be prepared in manuscript.

WAR DIARY
or
INTELLIGENCE SUMMARY.
(Erase heading not required.)

Army Form C. 2118.

Place	Date	Hour	Summary of Events and Information	Remarks and references to Appendices
RUDBROOK	15.10.17		Bn in RUDBROOK. AST	
BENNET CAMP	16.10.17		Bn moved to BENNET CAMP (A.4 B central, Sheet 28 N.W. 1/20,000).	
do	17.10.17		Inspections etc. AST.	
WIJDENDRIFT	18.10.17		Bn moved to WIJDENDRIFT in support to Bde holding WIJDENDRIFT Sector. Seven men gassed during gas shell bombardment AST	
do	19.10.17		Heavy bombardment. Several casualties. AST.	
do	20.10.17		Bn moved back to camp near ELVERDINGHE AST	
ELVERDINGHE	21.10.17		Bn in camp AST. M.O's report for week ending 21.10.17 Health of men normal AST Lt. J. A. C. Greene M.C. R.A.M.C. M.O. 17 W. Yorks	
do + Vee Bend	22.10.17		Inspections, baths. Battn moved up into Support of 105 Bde at Vee Bend. Cadey	
do Cadey Vee Bend	23.10.17		Battn in shell-holes in front of Vee Bend. Heavy shelling with H.E. & Gas. Several casualties. Lt Ramsden & 2nd Lt Sharp wounded. Battn ordered up to close support. On arrival there, ordered back to Vee Bend. Cadey	
WIJDENDRIFT	24.10.17		Battn moved back to WIJDENDRIFT. Continuous shelling. Working parties supplied to front line. Several casualties Cadey	
—"—	25.10.17		Heavy shelling several casualties. Cadey	
—"—	26.10.17		Bn moved to camp near BOESINGHE Cadey	

T2134. Wt. W708—776. 500000. 4/15. Sir J. C. & S.

Instructions regarding War Diaries and Intelligence Summaries are contained in F. S. Regs., Part II. and the Staff Manual respectively. Title pages will be prepared in manuscript.

WAR DIARY
or
INTELLIGENCE SUMMARY.
(Erase heading not required.)

Army Form C. 2118.

Place	Date	Hour	Summary of Events and Information	Remarks and references to Appendices
BOESINGHE – PROVEN	27/10/17		Battn moved back into camp near PROVEN. M.O.'s report for w/e 27/10/17 Colds & sore throats prevalent among the men. Sd. J.A. Campbell Greene Lt RAMC. Cadell	
PROVEN	28/10/17		Inspections & re-fitting. ~~Cadell~~ Casualties from 18/10/17 to 26/10/17 – 2 Officers Wounded. 3 Officers Wounded (Gas shell) 7 O.R. killed. 48 O.R. wounded. 45 O.R. wounded (Gas shell). Cadell Lieut & Adjt A.S. Cadman & Lt J.A.C. Greene RAMC to hospital, gassed. 2/Lt Stones & R.S.M. admitted for duty. Cadell	
—"—	29/10/17		Church Parade & re-fitting. Cadell	
– DE WIPPE	30/10/17		Battn moved to camp at DE WIPPE CABARET. Cadell	
DE WIPPE	31/10/17		Inspections & refitting. Battalion congratulated by G.O.C. 35th Divn for good work during last 2 tours in the line. Cadell	

[illegible] Lt. Col.
Cmndg 17th West Yorks Regt.

T2134. Wt. W708–776. 500000. 4/15. Sir J. C. & S.

11 Secret

To:- D.A.G.
Base.

Herewith War Diary of this Bn from 1st Novr to 8th Decr date of amalgamation of this Unit with 15th W. Yorks

J. H. Gill -
Major
Cdg. 17th West Yorkshire Rgt.

Instructions regarding War Diaries and Intelligence Summaries are contained in F. S. Regs., Part II. and the Staff Manual respectively. Title pages will be prepared in manuscript.

WAR DIARY
or
INTELLIGENCE SUMMARY.
(*Erase heading not required.*)

17TH (S.) BATTALION, WEST YORKSHIRE REGT.

Army Form C. 2118.

73/31 App Vol 31 Vol 21

Place	Date	Hour	Summary of Events and Information	Remarks and references to Appendices
DE WIPPE & BOESINGHE & ELVERDINGHE	1/11/17		Battalion formed into one company under command of Lieut Richard. Battalion H.Q. & Details moved to EMILIE CAMP near ELVERDINGHE & Company moved to COLDSTREAM CAMP near BOESINGHE. Cadell	
BOESINGHE	2/11/17		Battalion employed on carrying parties in forward area Cadell	
—"—	3/11/17		Health of the men good (Sd) E.W. Stone. Lieut M.O.R.C. i/c 17th W. York Regt. Cadell	
—"— & PROVEN	4/11/17		Battalion moved to PLURENDEN (Cadell) ~~PORCHESTER~~ CAMP in PROVEN AREA. Lieut D.C. de Lissa to hospital wounded (gas shell) Cadell	
PROVEN	5/11/17		Inspections. Cadell	
—"—	6/11/17		Brigade Inspected by G.O.C. 35th Divn. Work on the camp. Cadell	
—"—	7/11/17		Training & work on the camp. Cadell	
—"—	8/11/17		Battalion moved to PORCHESTER CAMP Cadell.	
—"—	9/11/17		Training & work on the camp. Cadell	
—"—	10/11/17		—"— Lt Col P.S. Hall DSO to hospital, sick. Major J.H. Gill DSO took command of battalion Cadell. Health of the men fair. (Sd) E.W. Stone Lieut M.O.R.C. i/c 17th W. York Regt. Cadell	
—"—	11/11/17		Training & work on the camp Cadell.	
—"—	12/11/17			
—"—	13/11/17			
—"—	14/11/17		Battalion inspected by G.O.C. 106th Infy. Bde, who took leave of the Battalion. Cadell	

A5834 Wt. W4973/M687 750,000 8/16 D. D. & L. Ltd. Forms/C.2118/13.

Army Form C. 2118.

Instructions regarding War Diaries and Intelligence Summaries are contained in F. S. Regs., Part II. and the Staff Manual respectively. Title pages will be prepared in manuscript.

WAR DIARY
or
INTELLIGENCE SUMMARY.
(Erase heading not required.)

Place	Date	Hour	Summary of Events and Information	Remarks and references to Appendices
PROVEN	15/11/17		G.O.C. 35th Div inspected & took leave of the Battalion Cadell	
ELVERDINGHE	16/11/17		The Battalion left the 35th Division & came under orders of C.E. XIX Corps for work on railways & tramways in forward area. The Battalion moved to ELVERDINGHE & relieved the 16th Cheshire Regiment in WELLINGTON CAMP Cadell	
—"—	17/11/17		Working Party supplied for work in forward area. Casualties – 5 OR wounded. MO's report for week ending 17/11/17. General health of the men good. No contagious diseases of any kind (Sd) E.W. Stone. Lieut. MORC. i/c 17th W. York Regt. Cadell	
	18/11/17		Similar working party supplied for Corps Tramway Officer. Tramway started from Rose X Roads towards Stray Farm.	
	19/11/17		Similar working party. Majority of Battalion bathed at ELVERDINGHE CHAU.	
	20/11/17		ditto	
	21/11/17		ditto	
	22/11/17		ditto	
	23/11/17		ditto	
	24/11/17		ditto. Church of England Parade held in Marquee adjoining Bn. H.Q. [faint pencil: ... health of men good (Sd) E.W. Stone Lt MORC i/c 17th West York R. Cadell]	
	25/11/17		ditto	
	26/11/17		ditto.	

A5834 Wt. W4973/M687 750,000 8/16 D. D. & L. Ltd. Forms/C.2118/13.

Instructions regarding War Diaries and Intelligence Summaries are contained in F. S. Regs., Part II. and the Staff Manual respectively. Title pages will be prepared in manuscript.

WAR DIARY
or
INTELLIGENCE SUMMARY.
(Erase heading not required.)

17TH (S.) BATTALION, WEST YORKSHIRE REGT.

Army Form C. 2118.

Place	Date	Hour	Summary of Events and Information	Remarks and references to Appendices
ELVERDINGHE	27/11/17		Similar working party on Tramways.	
	28/11/17		ditto.	
	29/11/17		Every available man not on working party the previous day was sent up for work on Tramways. The new branch line was commenced from Light Railway (Rugby Corner) to Rose Cross Roads thence across the road with three sidings to Broad Gauge Railway.	
	30/11/17		Similar working party. Cpl WEST and Sgt HEMSLEY were killed by HV shell at BN HQ. Intermittent shelling took place throughout the day.	
THIEUSHOEK	1/12/17		The Battalion marched from ELVERDINGHE to THIEUSHOEK via POPERINGHE N. SWITCH ROAD — ABEELE - GODEWAERSVELDE. Billets were good. No men fell out.	
MERVILLE	2/12/17		The Battalion marched from THIEUSHOEK to MERVILLE via CAESTRE - VIEUX BERQUIN and NEUF BERQUIN. The men marched well and none fell out. Good Billets were obtained.	
L'ECLEME	3/12/17		Battalion again moved from MERVILLE to L'ECLEME via ROBECQ. Good Billets were again found. No men fell out	
BARLIN	4/12/17		The Battalion paraded at 9.45 am and marched from L'ECLEME to BARLIN via HESDIGNEUL and LA BUISSIERE. Billets were not good and the men had little accommodation.	
ACQ	5/12/17		A march was undertaken from BARLIN to ACQ, thus completing the journey in which the men had marched exceedingly well, no men having fallen out.	
	6/12/17		G.O.C. 31st Division inspected the Battalion at 11.15 am. 70 men to be transferred to the "TANKS" entrained for ~~Tanks~~ Machine Gun Base Depot at 3.30 pm	

A5834 Wt W4973/M687 750,000 8/16 D. D. & L. Ltd. Forms/C.2118/13.

Instructions regarding War Diaries and Intelligence Summaries are contained in F. S. Regs., Part II. and the Staff Manual respectively. Title pages will be prepared in manuscript.

WAR DIARY
or
INTELLIGENCE SUMMARY.
(Erase heading not required.)

17TH (S.) BATTALION, WEST YORKSHIRE REGT.
No
Date

Army Form C. 2118.

Place	Date	Hour	Summary of Events and Information	Remarks and references to Appendices
ACQ	7/12/17		Battalion paraded at 10-15 am. Men for 15th Battn West Yorkshire Regt left at 11am, Band of 15th Bn played party away. Twenty men of transport personnel left for 15th Bn W.Y. Regt and 14 left for 16th Bn W.Y. Regt.	
ACQ.	8/12/17		Remainder of transport personnel transferred to 18th Bn W.Y. Regt. Health of men Good (Sd) [illegible] Lt. KORL 17th W.Y.R	

J.H. Gill
Major
Comdg 17th Bn West Yorkshire Regt

A5834 Wt. W4973/M687 750,000 8/16 D. D. & L. Ltd. Forms/C.2118/13.

www.ingramcontent.com/pod-product-compliance
Lightning Source LLC
Chambersburg PA
CBHW081545160426
43191CB00011B/1840